# REDWOOD WRITING PROJECT

# READING
# RECONSIDERED

# READING RECONSIDERED

**Literature and Literacy in High School**

**Dennie Palmer Wolf**

College Entrance Examination Board, New York, 1995

Dennie Palmer Wolf is Director, PACE (Performance, Assessment Collaboratives for Education), Cambridge, Massachusetts.

The College Board is a national nonprofit association that champions educational excellence for all students through the ongoing collaboration of more than 2,900 member schools, colleges, universities, education systems, and associations. The Board promotes—by means of responsive forums, research, programs, and policy development—universal access to high standards of learning, equity of opportunity, and sufficient financial support so that every student is prepared for success in college and work.

Researchers are encouraged to express freely their professional judgment. Therefore, points of view or opinions stated in College Board books do not necessarily represent official College Board position or policy.

Single copies of *Reading Reconsidered* can be purchased for $12.00. Orders of five or more copies receive a 20 percent discount. Payment or purchase order should be addressed to: College Board Publications, Box 886, New York, New York 10101-0886.

Library of Congress Catalog Number: 88-071688

ISBN: 0-87447-538-4

Printed in the United States of America.

9 8 7 6 5 4 3

# Contents

# Foreword

**R**eading Reconsidered is the first of several projected publications intended to supplement and further extend the College Board's Academic Preparation Series. The books in this series seek to stimulate thinking and discussion about curriculum and instruction in six Basic Academic Subjects: English, the Arts, Mathematics, Science, Social Studies, and Foreign Language. An outgrowth of the College Board's Educational EQuality Project, this series emphasizes that success attained by American education in providing access to schools must now be followed by equal success in providing access to knowledge.

Specifically, this book discusses the experience of reading literature in U.S. high schools. In so doing, Dennie Palmer Wolf considers in detail, and through close observation of actual learning situations, many matters that could only be hinted at in *Academic Preparation in English* (College Board 1985). The result is an essay rich in example of how teachers in many different settings help students come into possession of what the author calls "deep literacy." Though Wolf focuses closely on teaching practice throughout the book, she also draws on her extensive background in cognitive research to explain how some classroom approaches support high literacy goals and some do not. In an important way, *Reading Reconsidered* represents a major step in meeting what Lauren Resnick describes as the critical need "to take seriously the aspiration of making thinking . . . a regular part of a school program for all the population, even minorities, even non-English speakers, even the poor" (Resnick 1987).

ROBERT ORRILL
OFFICE OF ACADEMIC AFFAIRS
THE COLLEGE BOARD

## English Advisory Committee, 1987–88

Ann L. Hayes
  Carnegie-Mellon University, Pittsburgh, Pennsylvania (Chair)

Wilsonia E. D. Cherry
  National Endowment for the Humanities, Washington, D.C.

Kristina M. Elias
  West Hartford Public Schools, Connecticut

Raul S. Murguia
  High Technology High School at San Antonio College, Texas

Alan C. Purves
  State University of New York at Albany

Jane C. Schaffer
  West Hills High School, Santee, California

David Waters
  Isidore Newman School, New Orleans, Louisiana

# Acknowledgments

T his book is the result of the contributions of many people who care about how students read. Several programs provided the opportunity to observe remarkable teachers at work with their students. In particular, we would like to thank the Urban Scholars Program at the University of Massachusetts, where this work was inaugurated; the Pittsburgh schools; the English Department of Conard High School in West Hartford, Connecticut; the Commonwealth School in Boston; and the teachers and writers of the DIALOGUE program in St. Paul, Minnesota. Through the generosity of the Bread Loaf School of English, the Secondary Study Group of Greater Boston, the Central California Teachers of English, and the Chicago Council of Teachers of English, it was possible to talk to teachers about their accomplishments and frustrations in opening up literature to students who might not otherwise become engaged.

The book owes a number of its questions to its originator and editor, Robert Orrill. The members of the English Advisory Committee of the College Board provided time and thought as individuals and as a group. Other readers also contributed their criticisms, doubts, hopes, and corrections to the manuscript: Courtney Cazden, Austin de Besche, Howard Gardner, Judith Hodgson, David Lawrence, Miles Myers, David Perkins, and Thomas Wolf.

As is often the case, a number of individual teachers were more than generous with their time, their insights, and their stories. They gave the work breadth. They are: Marilyn Caldwell, Bill Cooper, Mary Cullighan, Terry Gellin, Lolita Green, Linda Helsand, Joanne P. Hoffman, Kathy Howard, Diane Hughes, Jean Kabbert, Phyllis Koppel, Margaret Metzger, Aria Muha, Cheryl Parshall, Marvin Petrucci, Dan Sharkovitz, Ted Thomas,

Dale Woodiel, and Dan Wyse.

Finally, the Rockefeller Foundation, through its Division of Arts and Humanities, provided both opportunities and funding for research, which nourished and perturbed the writing of this essay in important ways.■

# Why Reconsider Reading?

**A** great teacher, Kenneth Burke, once described the experience of being a reader:

> Imagine that you enter a parlor. You come late. When you arrive, others have long preceded you, and they are engaged in a heated discussion, a discussion too heated for them to pause and tell you exactly what it is about. In fact, the discussion had already begun long before any of them got there, so that no one present is qualified to retrace for you all the steps that had gone before. You listen for a while, until you decide that you have caught the tenor of the argument; then you put in your oar. Someone answers; you answer him; another comes to your defense; another aligns himself against you....The discussion is interminable. The hour grows late, you must depart. And you do depart with the discussion still vigorously in progress (Burke 1974, pp. 110–11).

This conversation, with its sense of belonging and contributing, is open to anyone, even to a 15-year-old behind a counter:

> I work nights in a cookie store. What people usually say to me is things like, "I'll take two chocolate chips, those two big ones down in front." But yesterday it was slow so I was reading Brave New World for school when this guy comes in. He says, "You reading that? You like it?" He starts telling me all about Huxley's ideas and his experiments with people who could see into the future. He's talking and the place starts filling up with customers behind him. I'm saying, "Can I help you?" and he's saying, "You ought to read 1984."

But this conversation is not one that many high school students—individuals with 10 and 12 years of schooling behind them—want or know how to enter. For many of them, literacy is eking out sounds or writing down 'facts, not questioning or reflecting. And even for those students whose classes break out of the mold of magazines and young adult fiction, literature often is titles, authors, and plot lines.

Why is this so? Some would say that schools are crowded with students who are unprepared to read literature closely or with curiosity. Recent figures suggest that as many as one in four students lives in poverty. Illiteracy statistics indicate that large numbers of students come to high school from backgrounds where even the most practical and necessary kinds of reading are not a part of adult life. By the year 2000, one in three students will be a member of a minority group. For many of these students, not just English is a second language, the ways of talking and writing that belong to school are also second languages (Gee 1987, 1988).

But it is equally true that large numbers of English-speaking, middle-class young Americans appear only technically, not deeply, literate (Hirsch 1987; National Academy of Education 1985; Ravitch and Finn 1987). Many of them seem unsure about how to enter and engage the complex, subjunctive worlds of novels and plays or the packed language of poems. They appear to read largely for facts or entertainment rather than to answer questions they bring to, or discover in, books. Like Huck Finn, they have doubts about "taking stock in dead [or imaginary] people," and so for them, books can only be assignments or antidotes, not revelations.

Clearly, on both counts, we have to take a very close look at schools: the books we use, the questions we ask, and the implicit messages we convey about the place of reading. We also have to examine the "culture" of English classrooms, asking whether we honor rather than examine literature; whether we encourage students to ask fundamental questions; whether our views of good readings aren't shaped by a particular view of reading that might be open to challenge.

But it is a mistake to witch-hunt. Literacy is a social phenomenon; its definition and its distribution shift constantly. As recently as the end of the last century, we urged schools to deliver "recitation literacy" to the immigrant children who filled the rows of desks. Their literacy was the ability to hold a book and reel off memorized portions of basic *American* texts: the opening paragraph of the Declaration of Independence, a part of the Gettysburg Address, some Bryant or Longfellow. With the coming of World War I and the prospect of large numbers of men handling new equipment in foreign countries, army testers redefined the ability to read as being able to cope, on the spot, with novel texts—to the dismay of recruits used to reading familiar or even memorized texts. Yet currently, that "extraction literacy," so revolutionary in 1914, looks meager (Chall 1983; Meyers 1988; Resnick and Resnick 1977). Finding out who, what, when, or where simply does not yield the inferences, questions, or ideas we now use to define full, or "higher," literacy (Resnick 1987).

The definition of who shall be literate also shifts. Questioning, reflecting, discussing, and writing have always been a part of literacy for talented or privileged elites. But they have rarely been a part of what we considered important for students who were not gifted or clearly college-bound. A classroom where young women, learning-disabled students, poor and minority students, all read (not recite) and write about (not copy) Shakespeare or Steinbeck is an invention that is only as old as higher education for women, *Brown* v. *Board of Education*, and rulings on the rights of handicapped students. Our expectation of high levels of literacy for many is a radical, hopeful, and demanding departure.

Since the definitions of literature, literacy, and who shall be literate change, it is tremendously demanding to teach students to read. It involves constantly unpacking our notions of literacy to make explicit skills we, as adults, teachers, or people for whom reading "came easy," too often assume. It also means regularly revising what we value enough to ask others to read. This is something like trying to see the surface of our own eyes. In the end, we face a series of hard and unsettling questions:

What is involved in reading well?

How can a teacher make this kind of reading available to all students?

What do we have to change, within the very fabric of schools and English classes, to make this kind of reading and teaching occur?

These and similar questions are the work of this essay. Customarily, in answering such questions we have focused on English and assumed reading. Here, reading is in the foreground, literature in the background. Not because literature is unimportant. If Emily Dickinson weren't both simple and elusive, if the line between memoir and fiction weren't curious, there would be little reason for reading beyond the level of decoding. Even if they are debated and unsettled, we know something about the literary issues. We know far less about how we teach, rather than assume, a kind of reading that will make literature speak.

Hence, this is also an essay about *how* to read. There is tremendous concern that we have betrayed the *what* of education, creating generations of both students and teachers who are ignorant of the works, ideas, and concepts that give academic disciplines their vigor and backbone (Cheney 1987; Ravitch and Finn 1987). But this essay questions whether that kind of knowledge is sufficient. Part of what a field offers students is a characteristic *way of thinking*. Just as there is an experimental method for physicists and the rigors of fieldwork among anthropologists, there is a way of thinking about texts that is centrally (if not exclusively) literary. Not to teach students these habits of mind would be to cheat them just as surely as if we kept them away from books written before 1900 and burned all poetry.

The terms used in the essay—"opening a conversation with a work" and "crisscrossing the landscape" of a text—are not the familiar labels from teachers' guides and research studies. They are metaphors that signal the intentional, avid, or aroused quality that reading can have. Perhaps the most recurrent metaphor is one of talk. That is because the notion of intelligence, learning, or reading, which motivates what is said here, is not that of an individual mind sharpening itself against the ideas in an essay or the figures in a poem. Instead, it is the image of Kenneth Burke's conversation: readers and writers engaged in talk that lasts and evolves. In reading, as elsewhere, Hannah

Arendt may be right: "For excellence, the presence of others is always required."

Finally, this is an essay about ideas; it is not a collection of lesson plans. Teachers are not mere practitioners; their everyday activities constitute values or theories in action. Consequently, teachers deserve to join in the critique and application of research and theory that are likely to shape their work. This, as much as arbitration over salaries and working conditions, is a part of their profession. Moreover, research and educational theory turn arid and distant without the information and insight teachers contribute.

We hope this book initiates conversation. Just as students underline and circle what catches their eyes and minds, we hope that readers will do the same here. Chapter 8 discusses sample readings and includes questions so that teachers can experiment with the ideas offered in the book. The essay concludes with a series of questions about the institutional and intellectual settings in which teachers work. These questions are meant to spark an energetic back-and-forth about changes teachers have made and those they want to pursue. ■

# CHAPTER 1

# Reading Reconsidered
# Language as Inventive

For centuries we have considered language learning a matter of imitation: no more than hear it/say it. We have also held a kind of slate-and-primer view of literacy, teaching writing as transcription and reading as decoding. But in recent years cognitive scientists, literary theorists, and educators have turned this view of language use inside out. We have come to understand that we are not so much good mimics or code handlers; we are, instead, active, inquiring individuals who make it our business to construct theories about language and fill out the meanings of texts. This new perspective on language has remarkable consequences for the way we think about reading—consequences that we can just sketch here.

In this reconsideration, language learning is more inventive than obedient. When a young child learns to speak, he or she puts together completely novel words and sentences as a matter of course—utterances like "two feets" or "Daddy gone." These "errors" point to learners' native inclination toward, and skill at, building theories about the way language works (Brown 1963; Chomsky 1957). (How do you form a plural in English? You add an *s*. Hence, stars, feathers, and feets.) This kind of theory building about language never ends. Suppose an adult takes up detective novels. As he reads, he works out the characteristics of sergeants and crooks, the structure of a typical whodunit, and a set of expectations about the hard-bitten, urban commentary of a Sam Spade or the urbane chat of a Poirot (Kintsch 1974; Rumelhart 1975). And our inclination toward theory building is rampant. When we hear stories, we form understandings about their structure and language that we use when we read; what we read informs how we write (Petersen

1988; Squires 1988).

But our capacity for invention exceeds the discovery of rules and structures. Even everyday language contains the play, metaphor, and shape that sit at the heart of literature. In their crib monologues and counting-out games, children play with the patter and rhythm of language (Weir 1962). Any five-year-old can push at the boundaries of literal reference: shoes lined up inside a box make a "pea pod," a trail of cloud is a "scar in the sky" (Winner 1982, 1988). This natural play and elegance of talk hardly disappear with early childhood. Many of us have an ear for incident (Labov and Waletsky 1967). A high school student talking about his ride back from a dance not only remembers, he re-invents a nighttime vision with all the tools of narrative:

> The brights hit the trees, then deer in the middle of the road. They were moving slowly, like fish in a lighted tank. I stopped the car dead and ran down the road barefoot, calling "Hey, deer. Wait. Stay." Softly. I just wanted to touch one.

## Language as Layered

Besides being inventors, language users are also jugglers (Bruner 1986; Jakobson 1960; Searle 1969). As a student reads Dylan Thomas's "Do Not Go Gentle into That Good Night," she may read "go gentle" as "go gently" and then return to the phrase puzzled. Until she decides what sense to make of this unexpected pattern, she may think quite literally about the print on the page. A split second later, she may move on to ask why poems have to make hash of ordinary language. If she sticks with the poem long enough to sense the mix of tenderness and rage there, her own personal or cultural memory may be unlocked—opening an album of snapshots out of her past and a tumble of images of children saved, protected, and delighted by their fathers (Holland 1968; Rosenblatt 1976, 1978; Slatoff 1970). With luck, the poem will resonate for her, recalling other texts (lullabies her father sang to her, bedtime rituals they had together, maybe *All My Sons* or *Death of a Salesman* (Eco 1984).

All in the same moment, she may reflect on her current sense for how she reads. She may note, for instance, that this time out metaphors seem less strange than they once did, but that now it is the tone of the writing that she cannot pin down. Her reading is layered. Far from simply matching strokes and dots to meanings, her reading is also a process of remembering, realizing, and not knowing yet.

## Language as Social

We have also discovered anew how profoundly social language is. As speakers and writers, we acquire not a language, like English or Spanish, but our community's version of that language. That version is not just a vocabulary and a grammar, but a way of being with others, and an envelope for thinking, valuing, and believing. The kind of language some students learn at home is quite close to that of schoolrooms and books—it operates as an exchange of information between strangers, it presumes literacy, it assumes a knowledge of (and maybe even a belief in) the stories and phrases of one very particular cultural tradition. Other students have learned different versions of language—versions that may be tuned to values like intimacy and community—and different myths or tenets for thinking about human experience (Gee 1987; Heath 1983, 1986). So, to join in the work of the classroom, some students have to acquire what amounts to a second language—the one spoken in schools and written in books. But just like a first language, these second languages are deep-running ways of organizing experience and expressing thoughts. Acquiring them can change how a student sees the world: sometimes opening new possibilities, sometimes threatening familiar ways of knowing and saying. This means we cannot assume that simply because our talk about F. Scott Fitzgerald or Herman Melville occurs in English, it is not foreign to students who come from communities different from those that developed and maintain the conventions for schoolish and literary conversations.

Of course, language is social in a second way: it is part of changing human culture. T. S. Eliot suggested that each time a new literary text joins the "tradition," it shifts and alters how we read all that has come before (Eliot 1964). Sister Carrie opens up the fierce, determined side of Hester Prynne, for example. Similarly, works change as the world alters around them. Langston Hughes's "Harlem" is a classic, not because it stands still, but because it exhibits new possibilities as different readers meet and probe it. Rather than being an artifact of the Harlem Renaissance, it has a different bite since the 1964 Civil Rights Act, when unemployment still remains highest among black youth. In that sense, literature is not a closed set of venerable works, but a shifting and lively tradition.

Similarly, our conceptions of what it is to read well are far from fixed. Just within the last hundred years our sense of "good" reading has shifted dramatically more than once. In Victorian times critics could and did describe good reading as an intensely personal aesthetic response, on the level of the work itself, which included excursions into the lives, minds, and times of authors. Selections for high school students were regularly prefaced with short biographies outlining the major trials and tribulations of an author's life. Only a few decades later, rejecting what they took to be aesthetic gossip, the theorists of "practical" and "new" criticism argued that readers didn't need the frames of history and biography. Critics like I. A. Richards and writers like T. S. Eliot redefined good reading as "close" reading. Like any physical object, a work had qualities that could be pinned down through absolute attention to just the words on the page. A good reader could detect the elegant, self-contained system of images and meanings within a work. It was that analysis and insight that were the grounds for personal response and evaluation. Our views of reading are shifting again. Semiotics, deconstructionism, and reader-response theory all argue that works of literature are inherently unstable or "open," being rewritten by each reader in response to that reader's personal history and the surrounding circumstances (Barthes 1975; Eco 1984; Holland 1968; Iser 1978; Rosenblatt 1976, 1978; Slatoff 1970). The written text provides only a point of departure. It is much more like a musical score always up for reinterpretation. A play like *A Midsummer-Night's Dream* can be a romantic comedy in an age of confidence in gender roles and marriage, or a much darker, ironic vision of fickleness for people who have lost those forms of faith (McCormick, Waller, and Flower 1987). *The Scarlet Letter* may be a tale of moral order in the nineteenth century and a parable of injustice for a twentieth-century or a feminist reader. Now a good reader has become someone who can articulate his or her experience of reading. Clearly, our sense of what it is to read well changes. What we learn when we learn to read is our culture's and our time's version of reading (Eagleton 1983; Heath 1983; Luria 1976; Scribner and Cole 1983).

## Reconsidering Reading

Reconsidering reading in these ways has many implications for the teaching of literature. First, anyone who has learned a language has years of experience building theories about the ways words work. Therefore, many students—not just a talented or an educated few   have the capacity to think about language. Having played with language, making stories and metaphors, many students—not just those from literate homes—have an ear for exaggeration, irony, and fantasy, which is a rich and firm foundation for reading literature. Moreover, students learn about language and literature in any number of theaters. How well students read is fed by the kinds of questions they ask, the nature of the discussions they are part of, the types of writing they do, and the sort of responses their writing provokes (Brown 1981; Brown and Palinscar 1986; Petersen 1988; Scholes 1985; Squires 1988).

If the act of reading is, in fact, a matter of thinking and feeling along any number of paths at once, we are shortchanging students if all we talk about is decoding or analyzing the structure of a text. We also have an obligation to recognize and educate other reading processes that frequently go unnamed. These include the ways students engage with what they read, their reflections on the reading process, and whether they think about books as comments on, or questions about, the culture in which they live.

Since reading is a profoundly social and cultural (as much

as a neurological or a cognitive) process, the smallest acts—reading assignments, comments on papers, questions asked in class—are infused with a teacher's particular view of language and reading. But many of the readers in any classroom may bring a quite different set of expectations and values to a text. Rather than presuming views and values, teachers might, and perhaps ought to, use their beliefs to challenge students to (as one teacher put it) "know their own theories and values." What is literature for? What is a reader supposed to do? Is it all right for a writer like Ernest Hemingway to offer cool, detached descriptions of war and wounding? Is Mark Twain's portrait of Jim racist? Is a poem that sounds like ordinary conversation doing what a poem should do? Grappling with these kinds of questions is not a digression but a part of acquiring a deeper literacy (Graff 1987; Scholes 1985).

Not only researchers and theorists are reconsidering reading. Increasingly there are classrooms where teachers, working with students who vary in their expectations and abilities, are rethinking how they teach literature and reading. In the past year I have spent many hours observing such teachers and students. I interviewed high school English teachers to understand how they enabled students to think and play with ideas as they read. Much time was spent with students, asking them to think aloud as they read their assignments for the next day and reading journal entries and essays they wrote. I interviewed them about what they read, what place it has in their lives, and what they find troubling, interesting, or hard when they read.

In collecting these observations, I worked chiefly with ordinary schools and average students. Nevertheless, most of the examples here feature active teachers and students who would think out loud about reading. While some of what they say is taken directly from classroom exchanges, other portions were collected in personal interviews. Consequently, what is reproduced here may sound more thoughtful than what floats out into the halls of Lincoln or Fitzgerald or King High. In this sense the essay is about what is possible, more than what is average. At the same time the observations are not always of exemplary moments; they are simply occasions when teachers and students wrestle with important questions about reading. Nor do these moments describe the fullest reading of a work or the "right" way to handle a particular issue. They are slices of classroom interchange rich enough to provoke discussion.

These observations are offered as a way of sparking discussion, not of legislating practice. Teachers know their own students, schools, and situations with an intimacy that makes them the unmistakable judges of which issues are most central and which ideas are most applicable. The particulars offered here are not part of some complete system for teaching students to read literature. They only suggest the kinds of climates in which all students might learn to read literature.

Across many sites and individuals, common ideas and approaches emerged. Many teachers argued, and a number of students demonstrated, that learning to read literature depends on:

- Taking part in a rich and varied language environment
- Learning how to engage with literature
- Reflecting on the process of reading
- Participating in an ongoing conversation about the ideas and traditions literature highlights.

In the remainder of this essay, comments from teachers and students along with observations of classrooms are used to explore how and why these approaches are powerful. ∎

# The Envelope of Discourse: The Making of a Rich and Varied Language Environment

**L**anguage is the stuff of any English classroom. Every teacher uses talk to manage ("Open to page 43, the second set of questions") and to teach ("Edith Wharton was a New Yorker"), but the proportion of these remarks, and whatever else is added, is a matter of choice. In making those decisions, teachers invent a dialect for their classroom. That dialect suggests whether language is a means of control, a way to report information, or a medium for inquiry and delight (Cazden 1988).

## The Quality of Talk

A student and a teacher look at a paragraph from James Joyce's short story "Eveline." It is the moment when the heroine studies a room she is thinking about leaving behind forever. The dialect this teacher and student speak suggests that reading is a matter of giving expected and known answers. Russell, a high school junior, murmurs his way through a paragraph:

> Home! She looked round the room, reviewing all its familiar objects which she had dusted once a week for so many years, wondering where on earth all the dust came from. Perhaps she would never see again those familiar objects from which she had never dreamed of being divided. And yet during all those years she had never found out the name of the priest whose yellowing photograph hung on the wall above the broken harmonium beside the coloured print of the promises made to Blessed Margaret Mary Alacoque....

*Teacher:* Russell, what is going on there?

*Russell:* It's talking about the living room at her house. It's dusty. And the things that are there. A harmonium . . .

*Teacher:* Which is what?

*Russell:* Like a piano? And there's a print, I think of a prayer, like one of those printed ones like Home Sweet Home that people put up on their walls, and a photograph of this priest her father used to know.

*Teacher:* Mmm, mmm . . . but what is Joyce doing there?

*Russell:* He's giving the setting for the story.

*Teacher:* Right.

Here a second English teacher talks with several students about another of Joyce's short stories, "Araby":

*Teacher:* He draws you into the disappointment. The first part of the story is all promise; the boy keeps imagining what the bazaar will be like. Its name, "Araby," "cast an Eastern enchantment" over him. But yesterday, Marcus was talking about how, when you get to the train ride, the story zigzags between promise and heartbreak. *[He looks over at Marcus.]*

*Marcus:* Yeah. *[He turns to the story.]* He talks about the train going, no creeping, by these ruined houses, but it goes over a twinkling river.

*Teacher:* And when he gets there?

*Denise [reading]:* "Nearly all the stalls were closed and the greater part of the hall was in darkness."

*Teacher:* What does that make you think? *[Silence]*

*Marcus:* I was at this state fair when I was about ten. I got lost and went down the back side of the booths. No lights— everything was like tied together and cheap. The prizes, like those plaster statues they give you, were lying on the ground. Like they were dead.

*Teacher:* When they take apart the set for a play or a circus, they talk about that as *breaking* down the set. The make-believe comes apart.

This second teacher gives a vivid sense of his own engagement with reading and his pleasure at the language of literature. Also, the way the teacher brings back what Marcus said and the way he builds on Marcus's mention of the back side signals students that their language is powerful enough to probe the story. He speaks a dialect that carries messages about exchange and interest.

## Questions

The kinds of questions teachers ask are equally revealing. When questions stick to matters of management and facts, they install a low ceiling on the talk that occurs in a classroom. When questions open lines of genuine inquiry, they can teach students to sense and pursue ideas (Dillon 1983; Wolf 1987). In fact, much of what we know about intelligence and achievement shows that the power of what individuals know depends, in very large part, not on the information they control but on the scope and originality of the questions they ask (Albert 1983; Sternberg 1987).

A second student has just finished reading the "Home! . . ." paragraph from Joyce's short story "Eveline." She looks up and waits for the expected questions .

*Teacher:* What is happening in that paragraph?
*Leona:* She's looking at a room. Her room?
*Teacher:* What's Joyce telling you about that room?
*Leona:* It's dusty. It has old stuff. Junk's what I'd call it.
*Teacher:* Junk? What's really in the room?
*Leona [returning to the text]:* Like dust, a . . . print, an old photograph.
*Teacher:* And?
*Leona [checking back to the text]:* A har . . . harmonium.
*Teacher:* Which is?
*Leona:* Don't know. An instrument?
*Teacher:* Where was your dictionary? Someone else, what's a harmonium?

Certainly students need to understand what they read in order to make sense of it. However, Leona wonders if Eveline sits in *her* room—a hint that she is curious about how to envision Eveline's world. Suppose the teacher had drawn out Leona's half-formed question and asked, "Do you think Eveline had a private bedroom?" Talk along these lines might have led to a recognition of just how the lives of turn-of-the-century Dubliners diverge from those of late-twentieth-century Americans—or even to the tricky business of using one's own life to draw inferences about stories.

When Leona sums up the room's furniture as "junk," she may just be dismissing the question. On the other hand, she may be hinting at her perspective on the story's events: her sense that the souvenirs and worn furnishings of a family's life appear shabby and useless to a young adult. What if her teacher had asked, "Why do you say junk?" Leona might have pointed out words like *earth*, *dust*, *yellowing*, and *broken*. She might also have pointed out that Joyce describes false things: a broken harmonium, a print of promises to a saint, a photograph of a man whose name her father can't even remember. Her teacher might then have asked, "Why those things, not a worn rug or a torn curtain?" In the wake of such questions, Leona would possibly have been a part of a conversation in which her original impulse gathered force and direction. Ultimately, she might come to see herself as curious and the story as worth investigating.

If Leona's experience demonstrates what happens when significant questions are not posed, another student provides an example of where questions can lead. He remembers his experiences in reading Hemingway's *The Old Man and the Sea*:

> We have to write questions about what we read and bring them to class. A lot of the time the questions are English questions, like why the old man talks about the Great DiMaggio. But one day this kid asked if the old man was a winner or a loser. Everybody had to get in. Some people said bringing in the empty carcass was like advertising to everyone what a loser he was. Some people said when the old man brings the fish skeleton into shore, the other fishermen see it and know they couldn't have kept the sharks off, either. And they see he was a great fisherman.

> I wanted the old man to be a big-time hero. I hated the part where he couldn't stop the sharks, and his hands were always bleeding, and he was trying to talk to the fish like his brother. I hated how that went on and on. And how it had to end with him dragging in the carcass all picked clean. All like, "That's *that*."

Forming questions led to a new perception for this student. Instead of accepting Hemingway's style, he asked about the rightness of reporting old age, bad luck, and defeat as if the writer had safely watched it all from a terrace above the sea, distant and able to say, "That's that."

Far from being beside the point, this kind of inquiry takes the student into the heart of reading. In *The Old Man and the Sea*, Hemingway presents not just what happened but an argument about how the world is. The reader has to be avid enough to enter and move around in the world as Hemingway makes it out to be. Having entered that world, however, the reader can pull back and engage in the argument about how the world is or the consequences of creating such a world. In taking that step back, the student moves from empathetic to critical reading. In fact, he comes close to what Robert Scholes writes about Hemingway's stories:

> As critics we need to confront both the naturalistic attitude—this is the way things are, people can't help themselves—and the objective detachment of the narration—this is the way things happen, I am just recording. That is, the critic must ask why Hemingway himself assumes the positions of naturalism and objectivity and what the consequences of such positions are in the world of human action.... (Scholes 1985, p.38)

## Discussion

One of the unique characteristics of classrooms is their public or open quality. The feeling of being on display can lead to silence and caution, but it also offers the opportunity for dialogue. The quality of that dialogue, however, depends on teachers' permitting and encouraging genuine exchanges—something more than teacher questions followed by student answers.

A teacher discusses an assignment from *To Kill a Mockingbird* with her students:

*Teacher:* What in last night's reading was hard?
*Student 1:* You know, how the kids are supposed to be like Atticus—good, I mean, understanding about discrimination.

But they're just as bad as anyone else. When they play those scissor games about Boo Radley, that's mean.

*Student 2:* Even when Atticus takes the scissors, they just go and get the belt and keep on playing their Boo Radley game.

*Teacher:* Is that what you all think?

*Student 3:* They were just playing. They didn't know they were being mean; they were too young to understand.

*Student 4:* Yeah, if you didn't know me and someone said I had gray, sticking-out hair and I'd been locked away in my house all this time, and I ate the walls of my house when I ran out of food, then you would probably believe that I was crazy.

*Teacher:* How is that different from people having heard all their lives that there are differences between blacks and whites? Are the kids any better than the townspeople?

The teacher begins by assuming that texts can be puzzling and that to know you are puzzled is the first step to understanding. She encourages the back anwd forth of dialogue, asking for other points of view. Finally, once students have outlined their positions, she challenges them to reexamine their ideas in the light of a new perspective.

## Beyond Consumption

In literature classes, we often make a fierce division that separates acts of appreciation from acts of authorship. As novices and onlookers, students are to read and write about literature, not produce it. But there may be costs to positioning students at the rim of literature. Often we ask them questions like, "Why did Frost leave that up to your imagination?" or "Why didn't Joyce tell us what happened after the boy left the bazaar?" The students look down or out the window—in part because they think of English class as a place to know about texts, not as a situation where you take the risks and choices of being an author.

But consider what might happen if students were to read like writers: Here a teacher reads aloud the struggle between

Beowulf and Grendel's mother, who comes seeking vengeance for her son's death. She reads the description of the mother-monster's serpent hair, her fish-scale clothing, and her fangs. She begins the account of the hand-to-hand struggle and then stops abruptly

> *Teacher:* I want you to finish the fight. Try for the kinds of language, the sound of it, even if you don't get the rhyme. Remember what you've learned about Beowulf and Grendel's mother.
>
> *[Pause]*
>
> *Teacher:* Let's read them aloud. Everyone listen, because we want to talk about whether they belong in the poem we've been listening to.
>
> *Student 1 [reading her paper]:* She reached out for him to crush his head like a tomato . . .
>
> *Student 2:* No, uh-uh, too ordinary. Tomatoes are out of the grocery store. Something more brutal.
>
> *Student 1:* What, like a rock or a boulder or something?
>
> *Student 2:* Yeah, better. It goes with their being in the cave; it's more primitive, like they would be.
>
> *Student 3 [reading from paper]:* . . . he pulled his sword but he missed because of how she lunged away.
>
> *Student 4:* No, no because's like that. They don't explain in a myth, you just see it happen. Bang.
>
> *Student 5 [reading]:*    and as he went up into the earth, the black sand was still steaming with his victim's blood. He broke the surface and the underworld shivered in ice.
>
> *Student 3:* Yeah, keep it. The opposites, they work.

This opportunity to write breaks down the boundary between consumption and production. It cedes to students the role of the writer. From that stance, students uncover much of what distinguishes the world and the language of *Beowulf*—its vocabulary, its primitive starkness, its images of black and red, heat and cold. But the detail and the insight of that discussion all hinge on a teacher's inviting students to risk authorship and on students who know they can gamble on "tomato" or "black sand."

## "But They Need to Learn How to Read"

English teachers have much more to teach than literature: grammar, the rules of business letters, and public speaking all jostle for time. Asked to make discussion or creative writing part of their work, they explain, "But they need to learn *how* to read."

But reading develops from different quarters. It is fed by the quality of talk, the depth of questions and discussions, and the opportunity to step out of the role of language consumer. For example, reflecting on her efforts to describe a room (see Example 1), a high school student comments:

---

*Example 1*

The apartment overflows, grows on itself and seems to pour out of the walls and onto the street. Not even the corners or bottom shelves are empty, they are filled with dusty pincushions, half-finished pieces of sewing stuck with a dull needle, fat colored pillows.

---

I had to read my description out loud in class. Then people talked about it. One guy said he liked the way the writing had the feel of the room—jumbled and crowded. Someone else argued with him, saying it was overdone. I was amazed. I knew I had just written it off the top of my head. It put me on the inside looking out. It made me think that's what happens whenever you read. You are on the outside and you go hunting for clues; you find some, you invent others. But you don't find the original meaning just lying there; you build it up.■

# Holding a Conversation with a Work: Showing Students How to Engage with Literature

**A** story like James Joyce's "Eveline" is always demanding, "Fill me out." When we read about the "priest whose yellowing photograph hung on the wall" and then later find out that "he had been a school friend of her father," we immediately make the connection between "priest" and "he." But the story demands much more. When Eveline makes it to the docks to go away with Frank, her terror rises at the sight of "soldiers with brown baggages," at the sound of the "mournful whistle," and at "a glimpse of the black mass of the boat." Those terrors may not immediately be ours. To have Eveline as a serious center of the story, we have to re-create her sense of panic by imagining a parochial Dublin, working-class people who rarely traveled, and the naïveté of the Evelines who lived there. Or we have to make her fears breathe by analogy—imagining whatever gives us a sense of promise overwhelmed by terror. The question is, "How do students learn to engage with literature in this way?"

## Opening a Conversation with a Work

If we want students to interact with what they read, it is critical to show them that they have the kind of knowledge and questions that are going to make a difference. A ninth-grade teacher comments:

> I use as much as a week to start a book. Take *Lord of the Flies*. One day I ask them to define good and evil and to write me a short example of each. I read aloud the pieces

kids say can be public, and we talk about the range of things that count as evil or good and the irony that even though good and evil are such basic categories, they're fuzzy.

Another day I ask them what they know about British boarding schools, and we talk about uniforms, single-sex living, and the forced community of it all. They surprise themselves with what they know even though none of them has ever set foot inside one.

A third day we talk about being shipwrecked. What do you have to do to survive? We make two lists—what would be terrible about living alone without adults and what would be wonderful [see Example 2]. By the time we have had these discussions, they are impressed with what they know and they are ripe for the book. And I haven't lectured them.

Time spent in this kind of prereading alerts students to the central situations and conflicts of *Lord of the Flies*. Because students contribute, the issues are phrased in ways they understand.

## Sustaining a Conversation with a Work

Even so, many students simply don't know how to do anything but read a text doggedly, word after word. They have no idea

---

**Example 2**

LIVING ALONE

TERRIBLE

LONELY

NO ONE TO DECIDE FOR YOU

NO ONE WHO'S DONE IT BEFORE

NO ONE WHO EVERYONE LISTENS TO

WONDERFUL

NO RULES

FREEDOM

NO SCHOOL

COULD LEARN ABOUT LIFE ON YOUR OWN

---

how to interact with a work over time, accruing a more complex understanding. Teachers who realize this invent ways to "scaffold" their students' encounters with text (Bruner 1986, Cazden

1983). Continuing to reflect on her work with *Lord of the Flies*, the teacher says:

> I get them involved enough so they want to go on with the book. I start by reading aloud to them; I want them to have momentum, not to bog down in all those jungle vines.
>
> At the same time I have to show them how to take hold of what they're hearing. While I read, they have a journal out and keep track of their impressions. But of course you can't just say that. You have to set them an interesting problem to focus on. For example, every so often I ask the same question, like "What is your impression of the kid with the blond hair?" Each time I ask it, they write down their current ideas. From class to class they can see themselves gathering information. Somewhere along the line, I tell them we are looking at what some people call characterization.
>
> I try to give them the kinds of strategies that will get them engaged. For instance, I try to get them to predict what will happen as we go along. A few of them will offer possibilities. We talk about why they think what they do. They begin to see how you muster evidence from the text. But equally important, they develop a stake in what will happen next.

## Readers' Journals

Ultimately, as one student put it, "The point is to get the conversation of the classroom into your own head." One way that teachers help students to internalize exchanges about reading is to ask them to keep a reader's journal—a personal, ongoing record of their reactions to what they read. In these journals, students pick out passages or issues that interest them and write short comments that do more than paraphrase or summarize. Instead, teachers ask students to react, evaluate, predict, and even criticize what they read. Example 3 (page 26), for instance, is a sample of one student's entries written in response to reading the prologue scene of Sophocles' *Antigone*.

Because journals allow, and even encourage, the expression of doubt, curiosity, and criticism, students come to recognize that more than simple comprehension or appreciation is relevant to reading.

## Where Are the Limits?

At this point a teacher could well ask, "Wait, is reading literature just a matter of personal remembering and responding? What ever happened to the text?"

**Example 3**

Thebes: What kind of place if this? It's hard to read without knowing what kind of palace – like king of England or pyramids

our King Creon: IF Antigone is part of his family why does she talk like she doesn't even know him?

no one shall bury him: I don't get it, why won't Creon let Etocles be buried?? It is too confusing not to know

We are only women: I swene is just looking for excuses

Now the long blade of the sun: The chorus stuff interrupts what's happening, they butt in, would like it better if the action just kept on.

Reading literature is much more than reaction. Rather, it is what Rosenblatt would call "a transaction between the reader and the text" (Rosenblatt 1978). Just as students learn to hear metaphor and irony, they have to develop a sense for what is slavish, wise, or wild in a reading. Since these distinctions are drawn differently in different communities of readers, teachers need to talk about how and where they draw them. Here an English teacher remembers a student who made him articulate the differences between "wise" and "wild" readings:

I had a student raise her hand after we had been reading in *King Lear*. She said, "We've been talking about how horrible Goneril and Regan are and I don't know if that is true." She must have picked up that I didn't think so, because she went on to remind me how I always wrote on her paper to "think deeper."

So I challenged her to do that, pointing out that she was claiming something no one else had ever said about the play. She started backing off. Then later, when the kids were writing, I approached her and tried to get her to pursue it.

I told her, "Anticipate the other side of the argument." I got her to talk out what those other arguments would be: that Regan was responsible for her father's death, that she and her sister were the cause of Cordelia's death, that they left the kingdom in chaos and brought on each other's deaths.

Then I challenged her to explain what, besides evil, could have motivated them to act the way they did. She began arguing that Lear was at fault. He played favorites from the start by treating them as outsiders. I was doubtful that this proved anything new and told her so. She went away and thought about it.

She came back, saying you could not put human moral judgment on people who have been reduced to a subhuman level. She pointed out the animal imagery in the play, saying how early on Lear speaks of Goneril and Regan as animals. I kept pushing, asking her, "So what does that mean? Lots of people in this play and others are compared to animals." She pointed out these weren't just any animals, but hated, brutal ones—tigers and vipers. Then she went on to say that Goneril and Regan never make any appeal to a higher being; they never talk about God or good and evil. She claimed that made them less than human.

She began calling the paper "Is Goneril Good?" But I still wasn't convinced. When I went back to her, she pointed out that because of Lear, Goneril is forced on a man she doesn't love and that she falls in love with a man she can't have. She used that to argue again, from a different direction, that Goneril is not responsible for her actions, that she is driven to acting like an animal because her father takes away her choices—reducing her to the level of the animals and turning her into "a viper."

---

As onlookers, we might ask whether the animal metaphors explain, excuse, or only describe the sisters' wickedness. But the point is how regularly, and over what a long haul, this teacher engages with the student, showing her what his questions are and being open about what it would take to convince him. He has, in this way, encouraged her to risk a reading of her own. Walter Slatoff describes this well:

> It would look as though texts themselves are in great jeopardy. They are. The moment we subject them to real rather than theoretical readers, they enter the actual world of human confrontations in which everything is in jeopardy. At the same time nothing . . . argues against the reader's obligation to try with all his resources to understand and feel the point of view, vision, and meaning of the work itself. Nor need such a pursuit be urged on the grounds of objectivity alone, for any morality which requires respect for the uniqueness and otherness of things outside the self requires that the same respect be extended to works of art. What I am saying is that real respect requires not a suspension or a withholding of the self and its full awareness but an exercise and offering of them (Purves 1975, p. 36).■

# CHAPTER 4

# Becoming Mindful: Encouraging Students to Reflect On Reading

**R**eaders hear voices. Even high school students think about *how* they read as they read (Barthes 1975; Smith 1975):

> We were reading along in *Hick Finn*, and we got to the Shepherdson-Grangerford part. I'm going along in it, reading about the living room and the front porch and the feud and I start thinking, "What's going on here? This is supposed to be a story about Huck and Jim on the river. What's all this stopping off to talk about these families? Why is this stuck in here? The guy knows what he's doing. He must have had a reason." It really bothered me.

There is a place for being bothered. Sensing what you don't know ("What's all this stopping off to talk about these families?") provides hints about where to reread, ask questions, or rethink your assumptions. In fact, research suggests that one of the ways skillful and less-successful readers often differ is in exactly how aware they are of that internal monologue about their reading (Brown 1981; Brown and Palinscar 1986).

It isn't easy to show this interior monologue to students, nor is it simple to show them how this kind of thinking about thinking informs reading. It takes introspection and risk. But unless we make these fundamental processes explicit, we hoard an important part of what we know about reading. It would be like teaching physics or calculus and never exposing the process of problem solving (Collins, Seeley Brown, and Newman 1985).

## Learning the Subjunctive

The world of literature is a subjunctive world (Bruner 1986), meaning that it is a world where what might or could happen—

in a room, a heart, a mind—flourishes. Students can be puzzled by how selective, playful, and even ambiguous that world is.

A high school sophomore reads a paragraph from Hemingway's story "In Another Country." It contains a short passage about the machine a wounded soldier pedals to get back the use of his knee. The student reads:

> My knee did not bend and the leg dropped straight from the knee to the ankle without a calf, and the machine was to bend the knee and make it move as in riding a tricycle. But it did not bend yet, and instead the machine lurched when it came to the bending part.

Quite accurately, the student picks up on the functional, plain quality of the words, which leads him to expect a straightforward world, without irony or contradiction:

> *Student:* That's bad. If his knee's all shot up, the guy could never push a pedal like that down and around. If he can do it, then his knee's not wrecked like it says.
> *Teacher:* Maybe not, but maybe what you have there isn't an engineer's or a doctor's look at the bike. Maybe it's how the soldier sees it—a contraption for healing.
> *Student:* Then why is he riding it? That's dumb.

Specifically, this teacher raises the possibility that the story works ironically, not literally: the machines do work, not in the obvious sense of being therapeutic but by distracting the men who use them.

A second teacher, hearing about this exchange, suggested another way the student might explore the differences between a literal and an imaginative rendition of the story's events:

> I'd have said "fine" and then set the student to doing just what he wanted. I'd have him rewrite the story so that everything worked. And I'd keep him at it and have him show it to other kids in the class—all on the bet that someone would squawk and say, "No, stop, you broke the story now."

Both teachers realize what Flannery O'Connor knew: "The fact is, people don't know what they are expected to do with a novel, believing, as so many do, that art must be utilitarian, that it must do something, rather than be something" (O'Connor

1957). They recognize that "How am I supposed to take this?" is a legitimate, in fact a fundamental, question.

## Groping

Thoughtful reading is only rarely a matter of flashy insight. More often it is a gradual, groping process. But students often witness teachers' finished readings, which may have been polished over years. Such polished performances offer no keys to putting together a reading. For that, students need to overhear another reader think aloud, much as a mathematics teacher might in order to show her students how to take apart a word problem. Here an English teacher works his way through a poem, section by section:

> Okay, let's take a look at Gary Snyder's poem "Above Pate Valley." [*The teacher reads the whole poem once through and looks up.*]
>
> Right away, it's how simple it is—short lines, ordinary words, plain dealings—that I notice. [*Now he begins to read a portion at a time.*]
>
> *We finished clearing the last*
> *Section of trail by noon, . . .*
>
> He begins right off as if we were there and didn't need to be told the details, like whether it is the Rockies.
>
> *High on the ridge side*
> *Two thousand feet above the creek—*
> *Reached the pass, went on.*
>
> I know where he is—a giant landscape, one that probably hasn't changed between the time the very first people were there and the time Snyder was there. Words like *last, high, two thousand feet,* make it seem bold, sort of heroic. There is the kind of listlike way it's put together. Also the way he holds back any details. Who is "we"? A "trail" for what? How are they clearing the path?
>
> *Beyond the white pine groves,*
> *Granite shoulders, to a small*
> *Green meadow watered by the snow.*

A contrast between the rockiness of the mountains and the soft meadow. And the way a word like *small* has been pushed out to the end of a line, like *last* up above . . . there's something about scale here . . .

Even in this short excerpt we can see how a teacher offers several concrete strategies for "cracking open" a poem. By talking out loud, the teacher offers his overall impressions, his sense of what goes on line by line, and his first stab at trying to pull the poem together as a whole, while not ignoring moments of hesitation or confusion. It does not matter if this is the best or the most complete reading of "Above Pate Valley." By making the gradual quality of his own reading processes public, this teacher gives students a sense of how they might proceed. Unless teachers take that chance, students are on their own to discover by accident or by osmosis how a work can be entered and explored.

## Crisscrossing the Landscape

Experienced readers know it takes several returns and much back and forth between the text and a reader's own thoughts to

---

*Example 4*

The <u>Last</u> <u>Christmas</u> — 9/26/87

Levi is smart, smart enough not to get killed. A survivor even when he was still in the camp.

True friends, Lim and Alberto, don't betray each other / willing to sacrifice for each other.

Breaking stereotypes — The German girl who gave them food for fixing her bike, wasn't an awful German. Within a couple million people there's bound to be some good.

History vs. Story: I took a course on the Holocaust and it was about the whole thing, this is about one moment. You get detail from the story. You get someone's feelings....

---

arrive at anything like a genuine reading of a work. The challenge is how to provide for that reappraisal and reflection in classrooms where time is often limited and students' reactions to going back to a work are often "But we already *did* that."

As their first work of nonfiction, a mixed class of ninth and tenth graders read Primo Levi's account of his life as a German prisoner, *Moments of Reprieve*. Students read each of the vignettes, writing down comments and questions. Example 4 shows a student's notes for "The Last Christmas of the War," a sketch in which Levi describes what happened when he received a package of holiday food in the midst of the starvation of a camp. The student's notes offer a detailed look at the way he became engaged in the process of evolving a reading of a work over time. This is a patchwork of comments that include everything from the student's reactions to characters to his reac-

---

**Example 5**

The Last Christmas — 10/2/87

I am used to ~~hearing~~ hearing about the Holocaust as a gory event, through adult eyes which are concerned more with the allies' success than with everyday events. Here you see the war through tiny details. He writes about all the thinking and planning that goes into rationing out a week's supply of candy. The war is larger, due to these tiny things. He makes you see this awful mix. Like when he takes of his hat ~~the tiny~~ to salute, trying not to lose the cookie crumbs hidden in it.

---

tions to reading nonfiction. Nothing yet stands out as central, consuming, or pointed.

Later, having read more and having talked about the sketches, the student goes back to his original comments on "The Last Christmas of the War." Reading over them, he finds a thread that interests him, a kind of path through the essay. He writes a note in the margin: "something about the details under everything . . ." This barely held idea crystallizes as he writes some additional comments about his original observations (see Example 5). At this point the student has an idea about the particular sense he can, or wants to, make out of "The Last Christmas." Of all the various observations that showed up in his original entries, it is this idea of human specifics that he wants to track down.

But he isn't working alone. His journal goes back and forth

---

**Example 6**

Why do all these details matter? What happens because are The points with made ? details ?

First Draft Notes

Levi expresses his feelings through seemingly trivial details. He twists these trivial details into much bigger ideas, and conclusions. He selects unhappy memories, and uses them to teach others.

---

**Example 7**

Second Draft

Primo Levi is odd among camp survivors. Even through he lived through the mud and the hunger and the fear, he doesn't blame anyone. His stories are of his experiences rather than his abuses. His stories are not meant as revenge for the past. Instead, he uses the little details of his memories to uncover the human sense in bad things.

---

between him and his teacher, who takes an important role in questioning and probing what is emerging about Levi. The student writes the first draft of a paper about the details in Levi. It is, in many ways, a catalog of sharply observed moments framed by the student's admiration for Levi's vision. In the margins of this draft, the teacher writes questions to prompt further thought (see Example 6, previous page).

In the second draft of the paper, the student pursues the question of details (see Example 7). It is at this point that the student begins to "do a reading." His early thoughts about details have become a trail into the narrative. He can now wonder about the importance of details in the mayhem of a camp. At a different level, he may have realized that reading is a matter of crisscrossing the landscape of a work. He has learned something about being curious enough to notice, about recording and reflecting on the pattern of his attention, and about pursuing a question or a point of view that is worth returning to, mulling over, and developing.

## Risk, Tempo, and Worth

The belief that we ought to be teaching students to think about reading carries at least three implications. The first is risk. Teachers should understand the dismay, the pursuit, and even the confusion that are part of confronting a new work. Perhaps each year they should teach a work they are reading for the first time. Moreover, if teachers are going to make the process of reading visible, they can't sit safely at the edge. As older, more experienced readers, they have an obligation to talk aloud about groping for understanding or reaching for a genuine reading.

The second point concerns the tempo at which we teach. Literature anthologies are fat, and lists of works to be read are long. When you should be reading *Silas Marner* or *Walden*, it is hard to imagine stealing time to talk about the process of reading, to reread a poem, or to rework an argument. But, as one teacher commented:

> You see, for me, it's not a matter of taking time out of the curriculum to send kids back a second or a seventh or a tenth time to rethink or rewrite something. That *is* the curriculum.

This entails difficult choices, notably reading fewer books for longer times.

Finally, if students are to learn to reflect on their reading, we have to offer them books worth entering, worth groping to-ward, or worth being crisscrossed. To the extent that we put trivial or watered-down reading in their hands, we are in danger of teaching them that literature isn't worth the work.■

READING RECONSIDERED

# CHAPTER 5

# Reading Resonantly

**B**ooks are not just patterns of language or plots; they are also comments on the world in which students live. To read in a literate culture is to join the conversations of your own time and place. The person who reads can make the world hold still long enough to look at it critically (Friere 1970). Or, as the historian Barbara Tuchman would have it:

> Books are the carriers of civilization. Without books, history is silent, literature dumb, sciences crippled, thought and speculation at a standstill. They are the engines of change, windows on the world, "lighthouses" (as a poet said) erected in a world of time (quoted in Bettman 1987).

As teachers, and adults, we make these claims. But what exactly do we mean? What is it we want students to find out about their time and place by reading?

Imagine reading a short story you have never encountered before: Richard Ford's "Communist." As you read, you recognize it is a story told in the voice of an adolescent boy, Les, living with his single mother "up the Sun River, near Victory, Montana, west of Great Falls"—a place where the names promise the elemental glory of some final frontier, but where most people scrape by on seasonal work, beer, television, and a few daydreams about going to college, getting rich, or at least leaving town. One afternoon in November, Glen Baxter, Les's mother's old boyfriend, turns up, offering an out-of-the-blue chance to hunt Canada geese on their one day of migration. Out on a high prairie "that looks like the moon—only worse," Les shoots into "a sound that meant great numbers and that made your chest rise and your shoulders tighten with expectancy." But the strange bounty of the hunting turns ugly. Les's mother taunts Glen that he's poaching, and later they quarrel over whether a wounded goose should be left to die or should be shot. In the end, Glen empties his pistol into the bird, pushing off "something soft in himself"—something that would care for the bird, the woman, and her son. That night, listening to the geese in the distance, his mother urges Les to remember he "wasn't raised by crazy people" and to "keep civilization alive somehow." He promises, but life actually takes the shape of hard-rock mining and no-paycheck jobs.

The story might be understood as an example of characterization or as an experiment in narrative voice. But it is also a turn in one of several long conversations that run through American literature and record our changing sense of who we are. Glen, Les, and his mother can be seen as the descendants of the folks who "lit out for the territories" in *The Adventures of Huckleberry Finn.* The places like Sun River and Victory seem not like thriving river communities, but remote places where the humor of Huck's scrapes has gone sour. Glen and Les's mother carry on the feud between the freedom of life on the river and the confines of the Widow Douglas's civilization, but they show us how, for Ford, the option and the dream of the territories have shrunk and lost their taproots.

The story also speaks about the tension and the snap of relations between men and women in a supposedly modern, egalitarian world. We watch an event as primitive as hunting provoke old notions of male and female. We see the difficulty of remaking ancient habits, even in a land of change and opportunity. In this, "Communist" speaks to and echoes other stories: *The Scarlet Letter,* "The Story of an Hour," "The Short Happy Life of Francis Macomber."

"Communist" is also a variation on a boy's initiation into manhood through hunting. But it collides with almost any sense we have for that moment: Telemachus stringing the bow or a Plains Indian boy beginning to participate in the dream community of his elders. This is a modern, not a mythical, version of initiation. The ceremony is impromptu, the adults are uncertain, and Les comes away knowing not the majesty but the stumbling, ambiguous face of an adult world. In this, "Communist" is like other modern versions of initiation—Faulkner's

"The Bear," Hemingway's Nick Adams stories, Joyce's accounts of adolescence in *Dubliners*.

This suggests that to read fully is to read *resonantly*, with an ear for the long-running conversations that comment on our history and ways of being. But for many students these conversations are—or seem to be—carried on in secret codes. They are not sure they want to or could join in. The question is how to make the conversations vital—and open.

## Reading with Memory

To read resonantly, a student has to remember what she read and has to be interested in building up a history as a reader. But as one teacher remarked, "School can be a hard place to do it. It is a place with no memory. First period, second period; Monday, Tuesday; ninth grade, tenth grade. Very little lasts or looks back." To make it possible to read resonantly, teachers have to demonstrate and insist on memory—on students' willingness to think back on what they read in September, last year, or in some other class.

A teacher does this when, in the middle of *The Great Gatsby*, she says, "Remember *The Old Man and the Sea*? Think about Santiago's dreams there and think about the dreams in *Gatsby*. What do you notice?" This call for recollection becomes all the more powerful when the questions and comparisons reach beyond the confines of a particular classroom to something read for another teacher in a different year:

> In *Weep Not, Child*, a novel we were reading about Africa, there is a scene where the boy's loincloth blows open as he is coming down the road toward a woman from his village. He is ashamed. The language is right out of Genesis and the Garden of Eden, so I asked the students, "Where did you hear this before? Remember in ninth grade, you read the Bible? What happened in the Garden?" Some remembered, some didn't. So I sent someone down to a ninth-grade room to bring back a Bible, and I read it to them.

There is a reflective side to this kind of memory. Looking back might allow students as readers to have a sense for their autobiographies—just as artists might when paging through their portfolios:

> Think what it would be like if students read *Lord of the Flies* as ninth graders, and then they read it again as seniors. What if they kept their journals, or papers, and could look back? What if I asked them to write about their development as readers—or if they did that for each other?

Two lessons might grow out of this kind of memory. The first is, "What you did earlier is not trivial; it is going to matter for as long as you read." The second is, "Reading is not some kind of fixed ability; it evolves because you read."

## Hearing the Conversations in a Work

At the front of his play *Ma Rainey's Black Bottom* (1985), August Wilson has put an essay. It begins:

> It is early March in Chicago, 1927. There is a bit of a chill in the air. Winter has broken but the wind coming off the lake does not carry the promise of spring. The people of the city are bundled and brisk in their defense against such misfortunes as the weather, and the business of the city proceeds largely undisturbed.
> Chicago in 1927 is a rough city, a bruising city, a city of millionaires and derelicts, gangsters and roughhouse dandies, whores and Irish grandmothers who move through the streets fingering long black rosaries. Somewhere a man is wrestling with the taste of a woman in his cheek. Somewhere a dog is barking. Somewhere the moon has fallen through a window and broken into thirty pieces of silver.

Getting ready to read the play, a teacher challenges her students:

> *Teacher:* Read just these paragraphs and talk about all the other stories those dozen lines trigger for you. Not so much personal ones like having been cold, or looking out a window at night. Stories you have heard or read.
> *Student 1:* Chicago and gangsters. The "Untouchables," the fight between good like Eliot Ness and evil like Al Capone. Quick getaways and bootleggers.

*Student 2:* I don't know what it is, something about the opposites: millionaires and derelicts, whores and grandmothers.

*Teacher:* Anybody, what's that?

*[Silence]*

*Student 2:* You hear it in church. It's music.

*Teacher:* What do you mean? Say more.

*Student 2:* The jumps from one place to another are smooth. It doesn't sound chopped up. *[Begins to form bits musically.]* Bundled and brisk . . . *Somewhere a* man, *somewhere a* dog, *somewhere the* moon . . . such misfortunes . . .

*Teacher:* Mmm, mmm.

*Student 3:* It reminds me of all kinds of stories of people landing in big cities, immigrants coming in.

*Student 4:* The autobiography of Billie Holiday. The way she gets beaten up by the city—that's the part about how bruising the city is.

*Student 5:* I remember a kid's book, a picture book, the moon seemed like a metal plate.

*Teacher:* What about this thirty pieces of silver?

*Student 3:* Like money.

*Teacher:* What about money?

*Student 3:* Silver pieces sort of reminds you of colonial America, that it is pieces of silver and not silver pieces.

*Teacher:* Anyone know the story of Judas and the thirty pieces of silver?

*[Silence]*

*Teacher:* One of his disciples, Judas, sold Jesus to the Romans for thirty pieces of silver. We'll read it before we get through the play.

What Wilson writes loosens memories of movies, children's books, the rhythms of church language, and biographies. Yet the play is built around a long-running conversation about one man selling another. It is a conversation that begins with Judas and Jesus, it touches the history of black and white men, and it damages the particular lives of the musicians waiting to rehearse with Ma Rainey.

Since this is not a conversation that students can hear easily or on their own, the question becomes how to make that knowledge available. What this particular teacher does is worth considering: She literally *shows* students what it is to notice and follow the network of references and ideas that thread through the play. She collects the works that the play builds on or speaks to—sheet music, essays by black writers like W. E. B. Du Bois, samples of Joseph and his brothers, the stories of Judas and Jesus. As they read the play, the students also read these other voices in the conversation.

## To Know the Tradition

There is also much talk and writing about another side of memory—how students lack knowledge of the history and works that make up a Western and an American tradition (Cheney 1987; Hirsch 1987; Ravitch and Finn 1987). But the idea of literature as a set of long-running conversations suggests that we may want to examine what it means to know a tradition.

Even the most traditional works—Shakespeare, Twain, Dickinson, Joyce—continue to evolve. Conveying a tradition is not a matter of indoctrination or vaccination. Old, familiar works are rewritten by new and different readers. Read in the context of the turn of the century and Joyce's other works, "Eveline" is about a failure of will, the inability to leave a familiar round of drudgery. But for readers who live in the wake of women's suffrage and feminism, "Eveline" *becomes* the story of whether a woman can invent autonomy in a man's world. Eveline rushes to the docks, but even if she boarded the ship, she would have the liberty of being Frank's wife in a place that isn't Dublin. This perspective may give the story a texture it never—or barely—had when it first appeared. One high school reader, talking about the notes she made in her copy of "Eveline," (see Example 8) makes this point:

> I was rereading the story, looking for an idea to write about. I was looking at the parts in quotes, where people talk. Her father, her mother, the woman at the Stores, Frank. But she is the center of the story and she never says anything out loud. She only listens and reacts. People talk to her and about her and she never speaks up.

*Example 8*

**EVELINE**

nue she could hear a street organ playing. She knew the air. Strange that it should come that very night to remind her of the promise to her mother, her promise to keep the home together as long as she could. She remembered the last night of her mother's illness; she was again in the close dark room at the other side of the hall and outside she heard a melancholy air of Italy. The organ-player had been ordered to go away and given sixpence. She remembered her father strutting back into the sickroom saying:

FATHER —Damned Italians! coming over here!

As she mused the pitiful vision of her mother's life laid its spell on the very quick of her being—that life of commonplace sacrifices closing in final craziness. She trembled as she heard again her mother's voice saying constantly with foolish insistence:

MOTHER —Derevaun Seraun! Derevaun Seraun!

She stood up in a sudden impulse of terror. Escape! She must escape! Frank would save her. He would give her life, perhaps love, too. But she wanted to live. Why should she be unhappy? She had a right to happiness. Frank would take her in his arms, fold her in his arms. He would save her.

.     .     .     .     .     .     .     .     .

She stood among the swaying crowd in the station at the North Wall. He held her hand and she knew that he was speaking to her, saying something about the passage over and over again. The station was full of soldiers with brown baggages. Through the wide doors of the sheds she caught a glimpse of the black mass of the boat, lying in beside the quay wall, with illumined portholes. She answered nothing. She felt her cheek pale and cold and, out of a maze of distress, she prayed to God to direct her, to show her what was her duty. The boat blew a long mournful whistle into the mist. If she went, to-morrow she would be on the sea with Frank, steaming toward Buenos Ayres. Their passage had been booked. Could she still draw back after all he had done for her? Her distress awoke a nausea in her body and she kept moving her lips in silent fervent prayer.

A bell clanged upon her heart. She felt him seize her hand:

FRANK —Come!

All the seas of the world tumbled about her heart. He was drawing her into them: he would drown her. She gripped with both hands at the iron railing.

FRANK —Come!

No! No! No! It was impossible. Her hands clutched the iron in frenzy. Amid the seas she sent a cry of anguish!    NOT TALK

FRANK —Eveline! Evvy!

He rushed beyond the barrier and called to her to follow. He was shouted at to go on but he still called to her. She set her white face to him, passive, like a helpless animal. Her eyes gave him no sign of love or farewell or recognition.

A tradition is a two-way street. It is an important store-house of images and ideas. But it isn't fixed. The pattern of quotes has always been a part of "Eveline." But this reader lifts them up, pulls them forward, and asks us to see them as revealing. What was once a detail becomes the new heart of the story.

Works also change in the light of new works. In "Communist," the Ford story described earlier in this chapter, Les witnesses Glen lose control and listens to his mother's dreams. These moments may bring back Huck Finn's eye for the chicanery and confusion of most adults. But rather than just echoing Twain, the experience of reading "Communist" could change a reader's understanding of *The Adventures of Huckleberry Finn.* He might notice, more than before, the irony of a land of eternal youth where the children, like Huck and Les, are older than the adults. He might also realize the essential steadiness that Twain's world possessed, by seeing that where Twain wrote in the Widow Douglas, Aunt Polly, and Jim, Ford left blank spaces.

Finally, a tradition can't become clear without contrast or collision. To understand "Eveline," students may need to read a story where the traditional world is beloved and where leaving is foolish—as in Alice Walker's description of the rural South in "Everyday Uses." The Walker story, with its talk of quilts and continuing care for an old mother, comes from outside the usual American tradition, where heroism is "lighting out for the territories." But without the contrast that Walker offers, that aspect of "Eveline" or *The Adventures of Huckleberry Finn* might be invisible. Readers rely on differences to make "the tradition" visible enough to be understood, rather than looked through.

## More Than Local Reading

Much of the time we teach students to read locally, attending closely to the ideas and patterns in a particular work. In doing so, we narrow reading, cutting readers off from recognizing the larger images, ideas, and cultural conversations that show up sharply when we look across works. To change this, we need actually to teach students how to hear the different conversations going on in works, showing them the other stories, images, or events they come from, much as the teacher did with *Ma Rainey's Black Bottom.* We also have to consider how to structure reading so that these conversations stand out. The consequences of this are simple but far-reaching.

To hear the conversations across works, students need a sense of their own reading history. Across grades and classes they must have occasions when it matters that they recall a story or a poem read earlier. Quite possibly they should keep readers' journals, saving them from one year to the next. Perhaps they can be asked to write their own autobiographies as readers using books, journals, and earlier papers as evidence. In addition, students may also need a group of works they all know. Far from being a plea for a national book list or a fixed curriculum, this is the hope that teachers in a school might spend time thinking about a core of works they want to be able to build on and engaging in frank discussion about whose ideas and which traditions should find a place. Ultimately, the sequence may include the expected myths and the Bible, but it might also encompass the contrasts provided by contemporary, African, Indian, or Caribbean writing. Finally, we have to engage new readers in exploring the network of ideas in *The Scarlet Letter* or *The Adventures of Tom Sawyer.* Like anyone who is learning, sometimes they will miss the point or misread a text. But if encouraged to read carefully and if given access to the network of ideas and other books, newcomers have the power to amplify and even to revise the way we read the most familiar works. ∎

# CHAPTER 6

# One Reader Reading

**H**andpicked examples are one thing; life in a classroom is another. Suppose a teacher faces a classroom filled with 20 students: some pay attention, some doodle, some did the reading, some did not. Suppose their books are open to a story that is hard-going: demanding, ambiguous in places, set in a world quite distant—geographically and historically—from the one the students know. Just how possible is it to teach this deeper kind of literacy we have been discussing? Since there are no national data (and since we are talking about literature), perhaps an account of one reader, one teacher, and one story can be allowed.

Clarissa is 17. Only a few years ago she came to this country from "the islands." At a large urban high school, her past English classes have been a steady march of short excerpts followed by worksheets. At home she reads the newspaper, magazines, letters, but mostly she reads the Bible and a prayer book she carries with her. This year, in an after-school program, she signed up for Mr. Petrolli even though he's "hard." He makes students read whole books—and write. With him, Clarissa has been reading in Joyce's collection of short stories, *Dubliners.* Among these stories is "Eveline."

As Clarissa reads "Eveline" for homework, she agrees to talk out loud about what she notices. She comes to the paragraph where Eveline stands looking at the room she is about to leave:

> Home! She looked round the room, reviewing all its familiar objects which she had dusted once a week for so many years, wondering where on earth all that dust came from. Perhaps she would never see again those familiar objects from which she had never dreamed of being divided. And

yet during all those years she had never found out the name of the priest whose yellowing photograph hung on the wall above the broken harmonium beside the coloured print of the promises made to Blessed Margaret Mary Alacoque. He had been a school friend of her father. Whenever he showed the photograph to a visitor her father used to pass it with a casual word: "He is in Melbourne now."

As she finishes the paragraph, Clarissa begins to talk, showing how her months in Petrolli's class have taken hold:

She used to be dusting and now she's running her thoughts over the things she knows, like even the things her father used to say. It is the right word he [Joyce] uses here, *divided*, because if he says, "from which she never wanted to go away," it would be very different. When you just go away, you come back. Divided—it is like an orange; you cut it [she makes a sharp, slicing gesture] and it will never stick together again. To be divided from the things you know, the things of your family, is to be lonely, maybe always.

She does more than take information away from the story; she also fills in what Henry James called "the gaps" in a story, using her experience and knowledge of the world. To begin, she draws inferences: it is she, not Joyce, who says that the room is really furnished with Eveline's memories. It is she who senses that a word like *divided* has been chosen among many possibilities and must signify a very particular meaning. She recruits her own experience and imagination to enlarge the literal text: drawing on her own life as an immigrant to argue that the finality of leaving is like the slicing of an orange—abrupt, almost violent, and final.

She senses something that draws *her* attention—this idea of what division costs. It gives a point or a direction to the way she reads the rest of the story: she wants to know whether Eveline will see the value of home and family before she forfeits it for some distant elsewhere. As she reads, her own copy of the story becomes a map of the play of that interest (see Example 9). As she reads, she tracks Eveline's moments of saying no or yes or maybe to the idea of leaving home.

Farther on, she finds and underlines where Eveline's father is described as "usually fairly bad of a Saturday night." Still later, she circles that Eveline had "to see that the two young children who had been left to her charge went to school regularly." She draws a line down the margin of the paragraph where Eveline's father clowns in her mother's bonnet at the Hill of

---

*Example 9*

### EVELINE

was a long time ago; she and her brothers and sisters were all grown up; her mother was dead. Tizzie Dunn was dead, too, and the Waters had gone back to England. Everything changes. Now she was going to go away like the others, to leave her home.

Home! She looked round the room, reviewing all its familiar objects which she had dusted once a week for so many years, wondering where on earth all the dust came from. Perhaps she would never see again those familiar objects from which she had never dreamed of being divided. And yet during all those years she had never found out the name of the priest whose yellowing photograph hung on the wall above the broken harmonium beside the coloured print of the promises made to Blessed Margaret Mary Alacoque. He had been a school friend of her father. Whenever he showed the photograph to a visitor her father used to pass it with a casual word:

—He is in Melbourne now.

She had consented to go away, to leave her home. Was that wise? She tried to weigh each side of the question. In her home anyway she had shelter and food; she had those whom she had known all her life about her. Of course she had to work hard both in the house and at business. What would they say of her in the Stores when they found out that she had run away with a fellow? Say she was a fool, perhaps; and her place would be filled up by advertisement. Miss Gavan would be glad. She had always had an edge on her, especially whenever there were people listening.

—Miss Hill, don't you see these ladies are waiting?

—Look lively, Miss Hill, please.

She would not cry many tears at leaving the Stores.

But in her new home, in a distant unknown country, it would not be like that. Then she would be married—she, Eveline. People would treat her with respect then. She would not be treated as her mother had been. Even now,

---

Howth. She did the same where Eveline's mother dies, wringing from her daughter the "promise to keep the home together as long as she could." She underlines this last sentence and places an exclamation point in the margin.

But as actively as Clarissa reads after months with Mr. Petrolli, she is still learning. The next day in class, she tries to describe Eveline:

> *Clarissa:* She's nineteen and she's thinking she is going to leave her room. It must be hard for a rich girl . . .
> *Petrolli:* How come she's rich?

Clarissa hunts down the sentence about Eveline's "holding her black leather purse tightly in her hand as she elbowed her way through the crowds." Other students chime in, mentioning Eveline's evening at the theater and the boat trip. Petrolli recognizes that they are reading the story as an extension of their own world with no sense that Eveline's Dublin was ruled by different economics or expectations. At that moment Petrolli pauses and talks about entering the particular world of a fictional work:

> Wait . . . what else do you know about Eveline's life? What about the dusty curtains and the broken harmonium? Why were there all those squabbles over money on Saturday? She's not rich. She lives in a different time when there were no plastic purses. Anyone who had a purse had a leather or a cloth one.

The class moves to the end of the story. Until those closing paragraphs Joyce registers the absolute details of Dublin: the bright brick houses with their shining roofs, the cretonne curtains, the colored print of promises. But the closing paragraphs of the story suddenly deny Clarissa access. There Joyce brings Eveline to the dock ready to leave for Buenos Aires with Frank, but he has her hesitate, writing: "All the seas of the world tumbled about her heart. He was drawing her into them: he would drown her." Petrolli asks, "What's happening here?"

Clarissa ventures:

> Here I think she is staring down into the water and getting very afraid. Maybe she has never been near the sea before. She is thinking that she will fall in . . . that Frank will pull

her in and that she could drown. So she holds on. She doesn't want it to happen; she is afraid of the waves, the sea, so she screams to him not to pull her.

Petrolli is quiet, letting other students talk:

*Student 1:* I don't get this part here at the end. What's he mean, "All the seas of the world tumbled about her heart"?

*Student 2:* She was keeping him back, so Frank missed the boat. He had to jump in the water. And he was calling to her to jump, too. To show that she loved him.

*Student 3:* No, they're just standing at the gate to the boat. She's just looking down in the water and it's making her seasick and she's mad at him for bringing her down there. That's why she doesn't go with him in the end.

*Student 2:* So why's he saying things like tumbled and drowned, if she's not in the water?

*Student 4:* No, she only feels like she's drowning, like he's dragging her along where she doesn't want to be.

Petrolli comes back to Clarissa and asks her again what she would say about those closing paragraphs. She turns to the last page of the story and begins:

*Clarissa:* Okay, she is at the boat, down in the harbor. And I think she had never been on a boat before, so she is full of surprise. It is too much for her, the water, too. She feels like she will fall in and drown right there. And Frank is pulling on her, maybe not so gently. He is wanting to be there, on the boat. She thinks he will drown her.

*Petrolli:* This word *drown*, what does it mean here?

*Clarissa:* To die in the water.

*Petrolli:* So she is afraid she will fall in or sink on the ship?

*Clarissa [long pause]:* Well, I was thinking this: "the seas of the world" could mean more than just that. The whole paragraph, even using the same words, could mean something different. Like in the Bible . . . deep waters, troubled water, that kind of drowning, drowning in sorrows. Or "all the seas of the world," maybe it is like all the people of the world—they "tumbled about her heart." She knows she is leaving the little area where she has been living, even though it's poor and dusty. She is going out into the seas of the world, all those strange people she is going to be with in the bigger area. They will surround her and she won't know them, not like home with her family. That's a way he would drown her, too. *[Pause.]*

You know how white people aren't really white like this? *[She reaches out toward the white wall of the classroom.]* The same word, two meanings. So drown like to die in the water and drown like you are stifling and you can see yourself dying, all alone, surrounded by other people, but away from your family.

In this way Clarissa tunes her reading midstream, learning to go from registered detail to metaphoric reading. Petrolli listens—as does the rest of the class—as she works her way toward this understanding.

However, it is not just the figurative language of "Eveline" that is difficult for Clarissa. The story both evokes and denies familiar story patterns (Mandler 1984; Rumelhart 1975). We read about Frank with "his hair tumbled forward over a face of bronze," his theater tickets, and his teasing, and we sense a romance, maybe of the Prince Charming and happily-ever-after kind. It is a pattern into which we begin to arrange the rest of what we read: the quarrel with Eveline's father and the escape to Buenos Aires. But it is a pattern that Joyce undercuts, freezing Eveline's will as she reaches the pier.

This is difficult, however, for Clarissa to see. A few weeks later, when they are finishing *Dubliners*, Petrolli and the students are talking about the abrupt sadness of many of the stories. Clarissa argues that "maybe the stories aren't really sad." She comes back to "Eveline," talking about what might happen after the story ends:

You know, Frank's going to go away. He's going to be there in Buenos Aires for a long time. And then one day, one of the ships will be going back there to where she is. And he will get on it and walk right up her old street to that brown house. And she's going to be there waiting.

She's still sad she didn't get on the boat with him. At first she might be turning her face away, but then she's going to give in and they'll be married.

Petrolli is about to say something when another student interrupts.

> *Leora:* No way, she is depressing. She's nothing. She can't even make up her mind to get on that boat. He's not coming back for her.
> *Petrolli:* How do you know?
> *Leora:* He's always talking about how Frank lands on his feet. He's up, she's down.
> *Petrolli:* We've been all the way through *Dubliners* by now. Does anybody get out?

Together they begin to talk, moving back and forth between "Araby," "Eveline," and "The Dead." Talking about the class later, Petrolli says he likes giving them "memory"—"just because they read it, they shouldn't forget it."

Clarissa is important in all this. She makes the point that this kind of active reading is open to, and important for, all readers—not just those who already recognize Dublin or figures of speech. But Clarissa's teacher is just as important. It is he who insists that students like Clarissa deserve literature— even though they may be puzzled by the Irish geography, Catholicism, and mythology that thread through a story like "Eveline." "How else are they going to learn to read literature, if you don't give them the real stuff?" Petrolli asks. Even at the outset, long before he knew Clarissa would read so wisely, he talked out loud about the search and reflection characteristic of deep literacy. When Clarissa mentioned what she thought about the word divided, he didn't say "Mmm, mmm." He joined the conversation:

> Clarissa stopped on the word *divided*. Did you ever stop to think what you can get from a word or two? Take broken as the description of the harmonium. It makes me think of having a tinny player piano from Zayre's. You buy it, everyone plays it for two weeks, then it breaks and no one really knows enough or cares enough to fix it . . . and it sits there invisible in the corner of the family room, a reminder of everybody's hopes they'd learn to play overnight, be a star. I read broken and say, "What would be different if it were just a harmonium along with the photograph and the list of promises?"

When Petrolli finds that Clarissa assumes Eveline is rich because she owns a leather purse, he checks her and pushes her to think about the aspects of her life that can and can't be extrapolated to the world of a fictional story. The way Clarissa marks up her text, tracking an idea, may come from the day Petrolli brought in his old college copy of *Dubliners*, joking about the maze of checks, circles, and underlinings from his repeated readings. The way she breaks through to understanding the figurative climax at the close of the story might not have occurred if he didn't understand the point and the power of rereading.

Petrolli insisted that Clarissa read "hard" literature. He also insisted that she read it well. Everything she said was not fine or right just because she tried. When she read too much out of her own frame of reference, or shallowly, he pushed and resisted and questioned. But there wasn't any shame. She was learning; he was teaching.

Possibly what happens for Clarissa is something like what the writer Richard Ford remembers:

> For me, reading Faulkner was like coming upon a great iridescent glacier that I had dreamed about. I may have been daunted by the largeness and gravity and variety of what he told. But he never puzzled me so as to make me feel ignorant, as I had been before I read him.... To the contrary. When I read *Absalom, Absalom!* those years ago, everything came in to me. I got something. Somehow the literal sense of all I did and didn't understand, laid in the caress of those words—all of it, absolutely commensurate with life—suddenly seemed a pleasure, not a task. And I loved it (Ford 1986, p. 76).■

# CHAPTER 7

# The Making of Reading

**C**larissa has had three years of high school English, but she didn't learn to read actively and deeply until she spent time with Mr. Petrolli. Her previous English classes were places where reading was assigned but not taught. What is it about education, schools, or English classes that makes this possible?

The sociologist Jules Henry, writing about schools, insisted that students absorb lessons about, as well as in, reading, arithmetic, and science (Henry 1963). Teaching literature is no exception. We teach *Death of a Salesman* or *Othello* and at the same time we are teaching "what will pass as reading," "how school is," and "what matters in English class." That moment when a teacher explains about Steinbeck, the customhouse, or the groundlings takes place inside a particular moment in the way we think about education; it occurs in a school and unfolds within the "culture" of the English classroom, as well. Each of these influences shapes—and sometimes misshapes— how we teach.

## This Moment in American Schools

In their book, *The Shopping Mall High School*, Powell, Farrar, and Cohen (1985) say that American high schools are run by "treaties" (p. 4). Students and teachers know that the amount of work, the level of commitment, and the nature of classroom interaction are matters of negotiation. These matters are settled not by what will lead to excellence or learning but pragmatically: What will the traffic bear? What will students tolerate given their doubts that literature matters and given their after-school jobs? What can a single teacher, facing five classes and responsible for over a hundred students, manage?

In any given high school there are classes where the flattest forms of school knowledge rule and there are rooms where teachers insist that students struggle hard with original questions. Students rapidly learn how the 45 minutes will be spent. In some classes they can count on little more than a quiz on the reading and then a review of the answers to those questions. To other classes they have to bring questions based on the reading and a readiness to engage in heated discussion about the ideas of last night's assignment.

For some teachers rules and quantified descriptions of assignments dominate, possibly because they avoid discussion by throwing everything into the incontestable arena of numbers and point systems:

> Write at least four additional entries in Anne Frank's diary. Each entry must tell about a separate event. Every entry must contain at least four complete sentences. (Ten points extra credit will be given for extra entries.)

Other teachers talk frankly to students about the engagement and the quality of work they want:

> Write three questions about "The Jilting of Granny Wetherall." The questions should go beyond the facts of the story. They should make you think.
> Write a paper that interests you about "A Rose for Emily."

Teachers announce their terms in the kinds of information they require of students. In some classrooms students hear and see only questions that elicit short, easily corrected, highly quantifiable answers. By contrast, in other classrooms debate on a question persists and students have to write papers around open-ended and difficult issues. Here, then, is one of Jules Henry's lessons. In many high schools students learn that reading in a tough-minded, thorough, or reflective way is not expected; it is just one option. Reading restlessly or resonantly is not a basic competence, only an elective.

## Inside a School

Just as museums and hospitals do, schools shape the kinds of human interactions that occur within their walls. Beginning in the late nineteenth century, when American public schools first developed their characteristic form, a significant proportion of students left classrooms for industrial jobs. There was a call, particularly from employers, for schools to be accountable for producing not scholars or informed citizens, but reliable workers. Texts, tests, and classroom management techniques focused, both implicitly and explicitly, on training students to be attentive, obedient, and quiet rather than inventive, questioning, and independent (Callahan 1962; McNeil 1986). Many basic school skills were defined in terms of doable tasks, not the complex and specific forms of knowledge characteristic of a particular domain or field. On the one hand, these techniques grew out of the mandate to teach raw basics to large numbers of students—a task earlier and more informal types of education based on apprenticeships never had to face. On the other hand, these same techniques yielded what has been called school knowledge, factual information distilled into formats like lists and tested with sentence completions or multiple-choice items (McNeil 1986). Reading is no exception. The original intent of reading instruction was to train readers who could reliably extract factual information from machine manuals, job applications, or the front page of a newspaper, the approach led, in practice, to the kind of reading needed to make sense of schoolbooks and to answer questions at the end of chapters.

Borrowing from the model of product assembly and behaviorist psychology, early twentieth-century educators and researchers also argued that even complex skills like reading could profitably be analyzed into subroutines, which would yield successful performances when assembled in order. The result is that we teach in bits. We teach lessons on drawing inferences or extended metaphors but spend little or no time demonstrating what it is like to be a reader juggling all those issues in the context of a poem. Our sense of what it is to read has become falsely sequenced. We don't discuss the ideas or the voice in Zora Neale Hurston's essays without first looking up all the words.

## The Culture of the English Classroom

As late as the nineteenth century, reading literature was taken to be a pastime, the pleasure and duty of an educated person. In universities in the United States and in England there was much resistance to acknowledging it as a field of academic study. Those who pushed for it argued that literature carried eternal human truths that had the power to uplift and instruct; thus, it belonged in the curriculum just as surely as did religion or philosophy. Matthew Arnold maintained, for instance, that literature could save a nation from having "its tone of feeling and grandeur of spirit . . . lowered or dulled" (quoted in Eagleton 1983). Several decades later, I. A. Richards claimed that the study of literature might protect us from "the more sinister potentialities of the cinema and the loud speaker" (quoted in Eagleton 1983).

But sheer worship can undermine curiosity. As one student explains:

> What is the point of analyzing the things in the anthology? They already made it into the book, so we know they are supposed to be good; so what are we taking them apart for? What I want to know is this: if I read Stephen King the way I am supposed to read Steinbeck, picking out all the goods and evils, and all the special language bits, does it come out the same?

Deference, apart from frank examination, deadens the senses. We cheat literature when we treat works as masterpieces rather than as experiments or questions. Students need help imagining stories or plays as literal work— pieces of writing animated not by perfect vision and certainty but by intentions, curiosities, and questions.

Literature's defenders also argued that it is as rigorous and analytic as any science. Their thought was that a poem is an object with enduring qualities that can be noticed, described, and analyzed in the way that roundness, redness, or heat can be apprehended and measured. The poem speaks for itself just as a quartz crystal or an armchair does (Richards 1925). The problem with this legacy is that reading can become frozen into received patterns or routines that don't admit to the personal or historical nature of actual reading experiences. It leads to the conviction that *the* problem with Hamlet has been, and always will be, his inability to decide. Or to the notion that there is *a* way to read a poem.

The culture of English also turns on the conviction that teaching literature is worthwhile, while teaching reading is remedial. When asked if they teach reading, many English teachers answer, "No, I teach literature. There is a tutor (or a reading specialist) who does reading." For at least some English teachers, reading is a mere skill and one that ought to have been "taken care of" in elementary and junior high school. To pause and explain how to take apart a story is seen, ironically, as detracting from the experience—maybe like seeing into the wings at a theater production. In part this may come from what teachers see of reading instruction—its emphasis on isolated skills in a rote or drill format. But even though prevalent, this kind of reading instruction is far from necessary. The earlier examples of teachers guiding the reading processes of their students (see p. 26) and of teachers demonstrating their own processes as readers (see p. 31) suggest very different, and powerful, ways in which teaching reading can inform reading literature.

## And Now?

If we want students to read deeply, we have to take issue with these conditions. More specifically, if the observations offered throughout the earlier sections of this essay were turned into a manifesto, it would urge these points:

1. Students must not come to high school without any significant history of reading literature. Throughout elementary and junior high school, students should read essays, letters, poems, novels, and plays. The structures, the subtleties, and the demands of that kind of reading should be learned gradually, continually, and deeply.

2. We cannot continue to create a kind of two-tiered literacy. To "basic" and "standard" students we teach the literacy of forms

and letters, newspapers and manuals. To college-bound or honors students we teach the literacy of essays and fiction writing, Shakespeare and Woolf. Ordinary students meet lectures and worksheets, while privileged and bright students encounter discussions and research projects. To the extent that we give students simplified texts in place of literature, teach them remedially rather than developmentally, or show them only how to decode texts, we actively reproduce educational inequalities. In this way schooling often extends, rather than extinguishes, inequalities in students' literacy learning.

3. To read literature well, students must read not just closely but actively— something we cannot assume. In fact, we have to learn to teach, not assign, this kind of reading. Its components are many. Here we have mentioned just three as a way of suggesting what might be involved:

   (a) *Holding a conversation with a work.* To enable students to gain meaning from what they read, teachers have to insist that students make use of their experience to fill out the meaning of a work and to raise questions about it. Throughout this process, students and teachers will have to discuss the dialogue between a reader's personal experience and expectations and the messages to be found in a text, asking what the bounds are on individual interpretation.

   (b) *Becoming mindful.* Students have to become aware of, and increasingly responsible for, the way in which they read. For some teachers this will mean explicit talk about the way in which reading literature differs from reading the newspaper or a magazine. It may mean sessions in which a teacher, along with students, works on a single passage, picking out difficulties and generating possible meanings. It will certainly involve teachers in establishing a classroom climate in which students reflect on themselves as readers—keeping journals, reviewing those journals, comparing what they take from an original and a later reading of the same work, arbitrating between wild and wise readings of a work.

(c) *Reading resonantly.* Students need peripheral vision as they read, catching the way in which a work is linked to other works, and the way it shapes and is shaped by long-running conversations within a culture. While many readers understand the rudiments of this kind of reading, teachers have to take an active stance in broadening and deepening the kinds of connections students can make. Teachers often have to teach students explicitly how to find and follow the connections to other works or aspects of culture. Teachers may need to consider how to sequence the works they teach so as to highlight the continuities and changes in the conversations that connect the writings of different authors. Within schools or districts, teachers should think about designing a "common-enough" curriculum to permit students to respond to the continuing strands of ideas as well as to the techniques and stories found in literature.

4. If students are to become more accomplished readers, teachers will have to grapple with the current extent of English curriculums. There is no way in which students can read the same number of works and have time to read in the demanding, complex way that has been talked about here. As individuals, or as colleagues, English teachers will have to choose among works, finding ones that afford thoughtful reading and encourage students to reflect on their selves, their histories, and their circumstances. We cannot substitute coverage for understanding.

5. If we are to broaden our conception of reading, teachers need modes of assessment (both informal and more formal kinds of tests) that reflect this changed conception. For instance, we must exchange multiple-choice or short-answer questions for students' class discussions, journal entries, questions, and essays. In place of their ability to answer who, what, when, and where questions, we must find ways to look at their willingness to engage with a text, their changing reading processes over time, their ability to form connections across works, and their power to generate insightful readings of their own.

# CHAPTER 8

# Resources:
# A Workshop for Teachers

Left on their own, essays are much more likely to gather dust than to spark discussion. So, to initiate the exchange of ideas, we have included a blueprint for a workshop or a discussion. In the preceding pages we have suggested that teachers affect how their students read in numerous ways: by using language in a vivid, inquiring manner; by showing students how to engage with literature; by making reading processes visible; and by inviting students to notice and understand the cultural conversations alive in books. In Appendixes A and B we provide a sample story, Stephen Crane's "An Episode of War," and an essay, Doris Lessing's "Events in the Skies." We invite you to use these pieces to explore how these approaches to reading work.

Since there are more points of discussion here than you will want to use in one session, you may want to concentrate on those issues of most concern to you. Throughout, we have included brief samples of responses offered by other teachers to suggest that even the most exploratory and informal replies provide interesting starting points for discussion.

## Thinking about Classroom Discourse

Select one of the pieces. Read it through, thinking about a particular class of students you teach. When you are done, write several questions you can imagine asking in class. Think of questions that would draw those students beyond facts to interpretations, or would prompt them to think in new ways about what they have read.

One teacher who was curious about the language of "An Episode of War" posed these questions:

This is a story about a man's being wounded. But Crane never says the lieutenant was shot. Why not?

Shortly after the lieutenant is shot, he moves his sword to his left hand. Crane goes on to say that the lieutenant "looked at it [the sword] in a kind of stupefaction, as if he had been endowed with a trident, a sceptre, or a spade." How does the story depend on this kind of jumbling and denying of expectations?

If I said that Crane admired war and pointed out how he compares it to a historical painting, and to the ocean, what would you say?

Another teacher, interested in the character of the lieutenant, came up with other questions:

Crane never says what the lieutenant thinks. Why hold back that information? Try writing in some of his thoughts as he walks to the field hospital. What changes in the story when you add that kind of information?

- Listen to the questions posed by your colleagues. What did you realize about the story from hearing these questions? What does this suggest about the place of questions in classrooms?

- How could you engage students in asking these kinds of questions? How could you use their questions for teaching?

## Opening and Sustaining a Conversation with a Work

Read through the story or the essay. As you read, keep a running list of the kinds of information you are bringing to the text. The list should include both formal information (for example, literary or historical knowledge) and more personal information (for example, an understanding of the human situations that are at the center of the piece).

After reading the Crane story, one teacher jotted down these impressions:

*The conflicting images around war*

*The war in the Crane story is the Civil War*

*What the life of a soldier was like in the middle*

*of the nineteenth century*

*Medicine at the time of the Civil War*

Another teacher wrote:

*The different languages of war—*

    *propaganda (words and pictures both)*

    *frontline reporting (the observer's view)*

    *war stories (the soldier's view)*

*How does Crane make use of each of these?*

- Share the different topics that members of the group listed in order to create a "map" of the range of information students will need to make sense of the piece.

- Building from that list, select what seem to you to be the three or four most central topics for students to understand. Working alone or in small groups, generate ways in which you might alert students to this information.

## Becoming Mindful

Typically we ask students to read in order to learn about the text: the language of the poem, the central idea of the essay, or the style of the story. But literature also provides a setting in which students can learn about the process of reading and about themselves as readers.

### A Stand-up Reading

We rarely offer students explicit examples of how a reader struggles to make sense of a piece of literature. More often, we simply assign the pages to be read. But, given a little showmanship and practice, teachers (or other students) can provide vivid first-time readings.

Someone should volunteer to act as a reader, choosing one of the Appendix pieces. The reader should read a section of it, pausing to make sense of it *as he or she reads out loud.* The point is not necessarily to be smooth or brilliant or correct;

rather, it is to give the listeners a sense of what goes on in the head of an experienced reader: what false starts are, how ideas come to a reader, and how a reader follows the thread of a particular idea from beginning to end.

Here a teacher talks out loud about the opening three paragraphs of Crane's story:

> Coffee seems like a funny way to start a war story. Rubber blanket . . . makes me think it was going to talk about sleeping and then it's the mundane task of dividing the coffee. Why is this so important, that the squares be equal, this great triumph in mathematics? . . . I am completely confused by the rest of the paragraph . . . the lieutenant cries out and speaks of personal assault, but I have no idea why . . . why am I deliberately not told what caused this? Finally it comes here . . . blood on the sleeve, but I still don't know the cause. Now a little more about what happened . . . he acted "like a man stung" . . . looks "sadly" at the woods . . . Why sadly? Here, finally, we are told about the little puffs of white smoke . . . I have to stop and go back and make a long inferring process about what happened to him . . . that he was shot from a great distance during a time of no combat . . . why are we told this so indirectly, why not just say he was shot by a random bullet from the woods?

- From such a demonstration, what emerges about reading? What might students take away from hearing people think aloud like this about reading?

- Ask a second person to read the same passage out loud. What emerges from hearing two versions of the passage?

- How could you include such explicit demonstrations and discussions about reading as a part of your English class?

## Crisscrossing the Landscape: Doing a Reading

1. Turn to whichever sample reading you have not worked with closely, and provide everyone with a photocopy. Read the piece through, paying attention to how you are reading. Mark the text to show how you "crisscrossed the landscape" of the story or the essay. For example, you might underline, circle, or

make notes to show:

- Where the story "began" for you (that is, where you first had a sense of what the story was going to be about for you)

- The way in which that idea continued to develop (that is, the pattern of points that caught your interest as you continued to read or the way in which you abandoned early ideas when better ones occurred to you)

- Where the story was most intense and where it trailed off

2. Look back over your marked copy. With your markings as evidence, what do you notice about the path you have cut through the story? What is the idea/intuition/question at its core?

3. Reread the story, putting your idea on trial. Using a different color ink (or taking notes), keep track of:

- New information that you noticed

- Places where your ideas changed

- Problems with or questions about your original idea of the story

For instance, here are some notes and markings made by a teacher as he read and reread the episode where the lieutenant struggles to use his wounded arm to put away his sword:

### First reading

*being shot for no reason*
*while doing something domestic, like dividing coffee*
*contrast between orderliness and chance wounding*
*this is story about war, pain, death — esp. randomness*
*this episode is about how senseless war is*
*[In his copy from the first reading, he has circled a series of words that signal this randomness.]*

### Second reading

*senselessness is in his mind, not just in war*
*how little mention of physical pain, all psychological pain*
*maybe story began before wounding*

*a long time ago when lt. became a person*
*who thinks the way he does*
*maybe not a story about war, but about a kind of mind*
*[In his copy from this later reading, the teacher has under-*
*lined words and phrases that show this jump from a physical*
*to a psychological description.]*

Using your marked texts and notes, discuss what you learned about the process of "doing a reading" (that is, how a reader finds, develops, and revises, or hangs onto, a point of view about a piece of literature).

With your colleagues, talk over how this kind of information might be important for students to have and how experiences such as the one you have just had might be incorporated into your classes.

## Reading Resonantly

Literature might be thought of as one big book in which later works respond to, and comment on, earlier ones. But all too often, under the pressure of time, we end up concentrating on the work at hand. Because of this, we may be narrowing the way our students read.

The Crane story and the Lessing essay are both about war. But they come from quite different points in a cultural conversation about the experience of war. What do you learn about each piece by reading it in light of the other? Thinking aloud about this question, one teacher remarked:

> You sense a big difference in the two pieces. In the Crane there are still fragments of the expectation that war should be grand. He has to undercut the idea that it should be like one of those giant historical paintings of generals and horses. Against that background, you sense how different the attitude in the Lessing piece is. There only children can see the airplane as mystery and promise.

Consider what other pieces you might ask students to read in conjunction with these works in order to bring out other conversations that move through either or both of them. Here are suggestions offered by a teacher:

What comes to mind isn't just literature. I guess I am thinking about things like folk songs, too. Imagine if you showed students Stephen Foster songs and songs from the Vietnam era—don't you think they would see something like what's in the two pieces of writing? Or maybe even war photography. You know Mathew Brady went to the Civil War battlefields and actually arranged the dead bodies for his battle scenes? Some of that had to do with the difficulty of traveling, but somehow it always struck me as saying something about the way war was then. Just think about comparing those scenes with the newspaper coverage of Vietnam, even of Korea.

## The Context Around Reading

As we have pointed out, reading is conditioned by the political and social context in which it is taught. The effects of even the finest teaching can be curtailed and muted when the demands of a curriculum, the rigors of a teaching schedule, or the educational climate undermine the work that teachers do. Consequently, it is vital that teachers consider how they can effect the conditions under which they read literature with students.

Working in small groups, read through the questions listed here. Select one where you have experience making constructive changes. Describe what you have done, what the difficulties were, and how you managed to make the changes stick. Use the questions that other teachers raise, along with their comments and suggestions, to refine your ideas.

1. It is in high school that some students encounter literature for the first time. How can high school teachers work with elementary and middle school teachers to see that students have a continual opportunity to read literature?

2. The English curriculum is too crowded. There are too many skills, never mind too many works to be read. What might you as individual teachers do, or what could the English department within your school or district do, to slow the tempo of instruction and consequently deepen the level of reading?

3. Many English classes often contain readers who read at widely differing levels. How do you include the slower students in the reading of literature?

4. Students can't learn to read resonantly unless they have access to those works that provide a background for much of literature and unless teachers help them to see how a work they read earlier is changed by, and changes, what they are currently reading. How could you and other teachers establish a "common-enough" body of works to be read by students between the ninth and twelfth grades? What issues would come up? How might you resolve them?

5. The kind of reading we have been talking about cannot be assessed by the types of short-answer questions we have come to depend on. Think back on your own teaching: In what other ways have you asked students to demonstrate their understanding of a piece of literature? How might these strategies offer models for assessing changes in students' ability to read?

6. Teaching in the ways that have been described here depends on teachers' having time to read, to talk with colleagues, and to think about the most powerful ways to present a work. How does your department or school district support teachers in these kinds of activities? How could these opportunities be extended?

Returning to the larger group, tackle these questions one at a time, discussing the strategies and plans that were developed in the smaller groups. ■

# An Episode of War
## Stephen Crane

The lieutenant's rubber blanket lay on the ground, and upon it he had poured the company's supply of coffee. Corporals and other representatives of the grimy and hot-throated men who lined the breastwork had come for each squad's portion.

The lieutenant was frowning and serious at this task of division. His lips pursed as he drew with his sword various crevices in the heap, until brown squares of coffee, astoundingly equal in size, appeared on the blanket. He was on the verge of a great triumph in mathematics, and the corporals were thronging forward, each to reap a little square, when suddenly the lieutenant cried out and looked quickly at a man near him as if he suspected it was a case of personal assault. The others cried out also when they saw blood upon the lieutenant's sleeve.

He had winced like a man stung, swayed dangerously, and then straightened. The sound of his hoarse breathing was plainly audible. He looked sadly, mystically, over the breastwork at the green face of a wood, where now were many little puffs of white smoke. During this moment the men about him gazed statue-like and silent, astonished and awed by this catastrophe which happened when catastrophes were not expected—when they had leisure to observe it.

As the lieutenant stared at the wood, they too swung their heads, so that for another instant all hands, still silent, contemplated the distant forest as if their minds were fixed upon the mystery of a bullet's journey.

The officer had, of course, been compelled to take his sword into his left hand. He did not hold it by the hilt. He gripped it at the middle of the blade, awkwardly. Turning his eyes from the hostile wood, he looked at the sword as he held it there, and seemed puzzled as to what to do with it, where to put it. In short, this weapon had of a sudden become a strange thing to him. He looked at it in a kind of stupefaction, as if he had been endowed with a trident, a sceptre, or a spade.

Finally he tried to sheathe it. To sheathe a sword held by the left hand, at the middle of the blade, in a scabbard hung at the left hip, is a feat worthy of a sawdust ring. This wounded officer engaged in a desperate struggle with the sword and the wobbling scabbard, and during the time of it he breathed like a wrestler.

But at this instant the men, the spectators, awoke from their stone-like poses and crowded forward sympathetically. The orderly-sergeant took the sword and tenderly placed it in the scabbard. At the time, he leaned nervously backward, and did not allow even his finger to brush the body of the lieutenant. A wound gives strange dignity to him who bears it. Well men shy from this new and terrible majesty. It is as if the wounded man's hand is upon the curtain which hangs before the revelations of all existence—the meaning of ants, potentates, wars, cities, sunshine, snow, a feather dropped from a bird's wing; and the power of it sheds radiance upon a bloody form, and makes the other men understand sometimes that they are little. His comrades look at him with large eyes thoughtfully. Moreover, they fear vaguely that the weight of a finger upon him might send him headlong, precipitate the tragedy, hurl him at once into the dim, gray unknown. And so the orderly-sergeant, while sheathing the sword, leaned nervously backward.

There were others who proffered assistance. One timidly presented his shoulder and asked the lieutenant if he cared to lean upon it, but the latter waved him away mournfully. He wore the look of one who knows he is the victim of a terrible disease and understands his helplessness. He again stared over the breast-work at the forest, and then, turning, went slowly rearward. He held his right wrist tenderly in his left hand as if the wounded arm was made of very brittle glass.

And the men in silence stared at the wood, then at the departing lieutenant— then at the wood, then at the lieutenant.

As the wounded officer passed from the line of battle, he was enabled to see many things which as a participant in the fight were unknown to him. He saw a general on a black horse gazing over the lines of blue infantry at the green woods which veiled his problems. An aide galloped furiously, dragged his horse suddenly to a halt, saluted, and presented a paper. It was, for a wonder, precisely like a historical painting.

To the rear of the general and his staff a group, composed of a bugler, two or three orderlies, and the bearer of the corps standard, all upon maniacal horses, were working like slaves to hold their ground, preserve their respectful interval, while the shells boomed in the air about them, and caused their chargers to make furious quivering leaps.

A battery, a tumultuous and shining mass, was swirling toward the right. The wild thud of hoofs, the cries of the riders shouting blame and praise, menace and encouragement, and, last, the roar of the wheels, the slant of the glistening guns, brought the lieutenant to an intent pause. The battery swept in curves that stirred the heart; it made halts as dramatic as the crash of a wave on the rocks, and when it fled onward this aggregation of wheels, levers, motors had a beautiful unity, as if it were a missile. The sound of it was a war-chorus that reached into the depths of man's emotion.

The lieutenant, still holding his arm as if it were of glass, stood watching this battery until all detail of it was lost, save the figures of the riders, which rose and fell and waved lashes over the black mass.

Later, he turned his eyes toward the battle, where the shooting sometimes crackled like bush-fires, sometimes sputtered with exasperating irregularity, and sometimes reverberated like the thunder. He saw the smoke rolling upward and saw crowds of men who ran and cheered, or stood and blazed away at the inscrutable distance.

He came upon some stragglers, and they told him how to find the field hospital. They described its exact location. In fact, these men, no longer having part in the battle, knew more of it than others. They told the performance of every corps, every division, the opinion of every general. The lieutenant, carrying his wounded arm rearward, looked upon them with wonder.

At the roadside a brigade was making coffee and buzzing with talk like a girls' boarding-school. Several officers came out to him and inquired concerning things of which he knew nothing. One, seeing his arm, began to scold. "Why, man, that's no way to do. You want to fix that thing." He appropriated the lieutenant and the lieutenant's wound. He cut the sleeve and laid bare the arm, every nerve of which softly fluttered under his touch. He bound his handkerchief over the wound, scolding away in the meantime. His tone allowed one to think that he was in the habit of being wounded every day. The lieutenant hung his head, feeling, in this presence, that he did not know how to be correctly wounded.

The low white tents of the hospital were grouped around an old schoolhouse. There was here a singular commotion. In the foreground two ambulances interlocked wheels in the deep mud. The drivers were tossing the blame of it back and forth, gesticulating and berating, while from the ambulances, both crammed with wounded, there came an occasional groan. An interminable crowd of bandaged men were coming and going. Great numbers sat under the trees nursing heads or arms or legs. There was a dispute of some kind raging on the steps of the schoolhouse. Sitting with his back against a tree a man with a face as gray as a new army blanket was serenely smoking a corncob pipe. The lieutenant wished to rush forward and inform him that he was dying.

A busy surgeon was passing near the lieutenant. "Good-morning," he said, with a friendly smile. Then he caught sight of the lieutenant's arm and his face at once changed. "Well, let's have a look at it." He seemed possessed suddenly of a great contempt for the lieutenant. This wound evidently placed the latter on a very low social plane. The doctor cried out impatiently: "What mutton-head had tied it up that way anyhow?" The lieutenant answered, "Oh, a man."

When the wound was disclosed the doctor fingered it disdainfully. "Humph," he said. "You come along with me and I'll 'tend to you." His voice contained the same scorn as if he were saying: "You will have to go to jail."

The lieutenant had been very meek, but now his face flushed, and he looked into the doctor's eyes. "I guess I won't have it amputated," he said.

"Nonsense, man! Nonsense! Nonsense!" cried the doctor. "Come along, now. I won't amputate it. Come along. Don't be a baby."

"Let go of me," said the lieutenant, holding back wrathfully, his glance fixed upon the door of the old school-house, as sinister to him as the portals of death.

And this is the story of how the lieutenant lost his arm. When he reached home, his sisters, his mother, his wife, sobbed for a long time at the sight of the flat sleeve. "Oh, well," he said, standing shamefaced amid these tears, "I don't suppose it matters so much as all that." ■

# Events in the Skies

## Doris Lessing

I once knew a man, a black man, who told me he had been brought up in a village so far from the nearest town he had to walk a day to reach it. Later he knew this 'town' was itself a village, having in it a post office, a shop and a butcher. He had still to experience the white men's towns, which he had heard about. This was in the southern part of Africa. They were subsistence farmers, and grew maize, millet, pumpkins, chickens. They lived as people have done for thousands of years except for one thing. Every few days a little glittering aeroplane appeared in the sky among the clouds and the circling hawks. He did not know what it was, where it came from or where it went. Remote, unreachable, a marvel, it appeared over the forest where the sun rose, and disappeared where it went down. He watched for it. He thought about it. His dreams filled with shining and fragile emanences that could sit on a branch and sing or that ran from his father and the other hunting men like a duiker or a hare, but that always escaped their spears. He told me that when he remembered his childhood that aeroplane was in the sky. It connected not with what he was now, a sober modern man living in a large town, but with the tales and songs of his people, for it was not real, not something to be brought down to earth and touched.

When he was about nine his family went to live with relatives near a village that was larger than either the handful of huts in the bush or the 'town' where they had sometimes bought a little sugar or tea or a piece of cloth. There the black people worked in a small gold mine. He learned that twice a week an aeroplane landed in the bush on a strip of cleared land, unloaded parcels, mail and sometimes a person, and then flew off. He was by now going to a mission school. He walked there with his elder brother and his younger sister every morning, leaving at six to get there at eight, then walked back in the afternoon. Later, when he measured distances not by the time it took to cover them, but by the miles, yards and feet he learned in school, he knew he walked eight miles to school and eight back.

This school was his gateway to the life of riches and plenty enjoyed by white people. This is how he saw it. Motor cars, bicycles, the goods in the shops, clothes—all these things would be his if he did well at school. School had to come first, but on Saturdays and Sundays and holidays he went stealthily to the edge of the airstrip, sometimes with his brother and sister, and crouched there waiting for the little plane. The first time he saw a man jump down out of its high uptilted front his heart stopped, then it thundered, and he raced shouting exuberantly into the bush. He had not before understood that this apparition of the skies, like a moth but made out of some substance unknown to him, had a person in it; a young white man, like the storemen or the foremen in the mines. In the village of his early child-hood he had played with grasshoppers, pretending they were aeroplanes. Now he made little planes out of the silver paper that came in the packets of cigarettes that were too expensive for his people to smoke.

With these infant models in his hands the aeroplane seemed close to him, and he crept out of the bush to reach out and touch it, but the pilot saw him, shouted at him—and so he ran away. In his mind was a region of confusion, doubt and delight mixed, and this was the distance between himself and the plane. He never said to himself, 'I could become a pilot when I grow up.' On the practical level what he dreamed of was a bicycle, but they cost so much— five pounds—that his father, who had one, would need a year to get it paid off. (His father had become a storeman in a mine shop, and that job, and the move to this new place, was to enable his children to go to school and enter the new world.) No, what that aeroplane meant was wonder, a dazzlement of possibilities, but they were all unclear. When he saw that aeroplane on the landing strip or, later, that one or another in the skies, it made him dream of how he would get on his bicycle when he had one, and race along the paths of the bush so fast that . . .

When he had finished four years at school he could have left. He already had more schooling than most of the children of his country at that time. He could read a little, write a little and do sums rather well. With these skills he could get a job as a boss boy or perhaps working in a shop. But this is not what his father wanted. Because these children were clever, they had been invited to attend another mission school, and the fees meant the father had to work not only at the store job in the day time, but at night as a watchman. And they, the children, did odd jobs at weekends and through holidays, running errands, selling fruit at the back doors of white houses with their mother. They all worked and worked; and, again, walking to and from the new school took the children four hours of every day. (I once knew a man from Czechoslovakia who said he walked six miles to school and six miles back in snow or heat or rain, because he was a poor boy, one of eleven children, and this is what he had to do to get an education. He became a doctor.)

This man, the African, at last finished school. He had understood the nature of the cloudy region in his mind where the aeroplane still lived. He had seen much larger planes. He knew now the shining creature of his childhood was nothing compared to the monsters that went to the big airports in the cities. A war had come and gone, and he had read in the newspapers of great battles in Europe and the East, and he understood what aeroplanes could be used for. The war had not made much difference to him and his family. Then his country, which until then had been loosely ruled by Britain in a way that affected him personally very little (and he knew this was unlike some of the countries further south) became independent and had a black government. By now the family lived in the capital of the country. They had a two-roomed house in a township. This move, too, this bettering, was for the children. Now the brother took a job in a store as a clerk, and the sister was a nurse in the hospital, but he decided to go on learning. At last he became an accountant and understood the modern world and what had separated that poor black child he had been from the aeroplane. These days he might smile at his early imaginings, but he loved them. He still loved the little aeroplane. He said to himself: "It was never possible for me to fly an aeroplane, it never occurred to me, because black men did not become pilots. But my son . . ."

His son, brought up in a town where aeroplanes came and went every day, said, "Who wants to be a pilot? What a life!" He decided to be a lawyer, and that is what he is.

My friend, who told me all this, said, "My son would never understand, never in his life, what that little plane meant to me and the kids in the bush."

But I understood. On the farm where I grew up, once a week I watched a small aeroplane appear, coming from the direction of the city. It descended over the ridge into the bush on to the airstrip of the Mandora Mine, a Lonrho mine. I was transported with delight and longing. In those days ordinary people did not fly. A lucky child might be taken up for a "flip" around the sky, price five pounds. It was a lot of money, and I did not fly for years.

Last year I met a little Afghan girl, a refugee with her family in Pakistan. She had lived in a village that had water running through it from the mountains, and it had orchards and fields, and all her family and her relatives were there. Sometimes a plane crossed the sky from one of the larger cities of Afghanistan to another. She would run to the edge of the village to get nearer to that shining thing in the sky, and stand with her hands cradling her head as she stared up . . . up . . . up . . . Or she called to her mother, "An aeroplane, look!"

And then the Russians invaded, and one day the visiting aeroplane was a gunship. It thundered over her village, dropped its bombs and flew off. The house she had lived in all her days was rubble, and her mother and her little brother were dead. So were several of her relatives. And as she walked across the mountains with her father, her uncle, her aunt and her three surviving cousins, they were bombed by the helicopters and the planes, so that more people died. Now, living in exile in the refugee camp, when she thinks of the skies of her country she knows they are full of aircraft, day and night, and the little plane that flew over her village with the sunlight shining on its wings seems like something she once imagined, a childish dream.∎

Albert, R. S., ed. 1983. *Genius and Eminence*. New York: Pergamon.

Barthes, R. 1975. *The Pleasure of the Text*. New York: Farrar, Straus and Giroux.

Bettman, O. 1987. *The Delights of Reading*. Boston: Godine.

Brown, A. L. 1981. "Metacognition: The Development of Selective Attention Strategies for Learning from Texts." In *Directions in Reading: Research and Instruction*, ed. M. L. Kamil. Washington, D.C.: The National Reading Conference.

Brown, A. L., and A. S. Palinscar. 1986. *Guided, Cooperative Learning and Individual Knowledge Acquisition*. Technical Report 372, Champaign, Ill.: Center for the Study of Reading.

Brown, R. 1963. *A First Language*. Cambridge, Mass.: Harvard University Press.

Bruner, J. 1986. *Actual Minds, Possible Worlds*. Cambridge, Mass.: Harvard University Press.

Burke, K. 1974. *Philosophy of Literary Form*. Berkeley and Los Angeles: University of California Press.

Callahan, E. 1962. *Education and the Cult of Efficiency*. Chicago: University of Chicago Press.

Cazden, C. B. 1983. "Peekaboo as an Instructional Model: Discourse Development at School and at Home." In *The Sociogenesis of Language and Human Conduct: A Multidisciplinary Book of Readings*, ed. B. Bain. New York: Plenum.

— —.1988. *Classroom Discourse: The Language of Teaching and Learning*. Portsmouth, N.H.: Heinemann.

Chall, J. 1983. *Stages of Reading Development*. New York: McGraw-Hill.

Cheney, L. 1987. *American Memory: A Report on the Humanities in the Nation's Public Schools*. Washington, D.C.: National Endowment for the Humanities.

Chomsky, N. 1957. *Syntactic Structures*. The Hague: Mouton.

Collins, A., J. Seeley Brown, and S. Newman. 1985. "Cognitive Apprenticeship: Teaching the Craft of Reading, Writing, and Mathematics." In *Cognition and Instruction: Issues and Agendas*, ed. L. Resnick. Hillsdale, N.J.: Erlbaum.

Dillon, J. T. 1983. *Teaching and the Art of Questioning.* Bloomington, Ind.: Phi Delta Kappa Education Foundation.

Eagleton, T. 1983. *Literary Theory: An Introduction.* Oxford: Basil Blackwell.

Eco, U. 1984. *The Role of the Reader: Explorations in the Semiotics of Text.* Bloomington: University of Indiana Press.

Eliot, T. S. 1964. *Selected Essays.* New York: Harcourt, Brace and World.

Ford, R. 1986. "The Three Kings." In *The Graywolf Annual Three: Essays, Memoirs, and Reflections,* ed. S. Walker. St. Paul, Minn.: Graywolf Press.

Friere, P. 1970. *Cultural Action for Freedom.* Monograph Series 1. *Harvard Educational Review.*

Gee, J. P. 1987. "What Is Literacy?" Paper presented at Mailman Family Foundation Conference on Families and Literacy. Harvard Graduate School of Education. March 6–7.

——.1988. The Legacies of Literacy: From Plato to Friere through Harvey Graff. *Harvard Educational Review* 58(2): 195–212.

Graff, G. 1987. *Professing Literature: An Institutional History.* Chicago: University of Chicago Press.

Heath, S. B. 1983. *Ways with Words.* New York: Cambridge University Press.

——.1986. "Taking a Cross-cultural Look at Narratives. *Topics in Language Disorders* 7(1): 84–94.

Henry, J. 1963. *Culture Against Man.* New York: Random House.

Hirsch, E. D., Jr. 1987. *Cultural Literacy: What Every American Needs to Know.* Boston: Houghton Mifflin.

Holland, N. 1968. *The Dynamics of Literary Response.* New York: Oxford University Press.

Iser, W. 1978. *The Act of Reading.* Baltimore: Johns Hopkins University Press.

Jakobson, R. 1960. "Linguistics and Poetics." In *Style in Language,* ed. T. Sebeok. Cambridge: MIT Press.

Joyce, James. 1967. *Dubliners.* Harmondsworth, Middlesex, England: Penguin Books.

Kintsch, W. 1974. *The Representation of Meaning in Memory.* Hillsdale, N.J.: Erlbaum.

Labov, W., and J. Waletsky. 1967. "Narrative Analysis: Oral Versions of Personal Experience." In *Essays on the Verbal and Visual Arts,* ed. J. Helm. Seattle: University of Washington Press.

Luria, A. R. 1976. *Cognitive Development: Its Cultural and Social Foundations.* Cambridge, Mass.: Harvard University Press.

McCormick, K., G. Waller, and L. Flower. 1987. *Reading Texts.* Lexington, Mass.: D. C. Heath.

McNeil, L. 1986. *The Contradictions of Control: School Structure and School Knowledge.* New York: Routledge and Kegan Paul.

Mandler, J. 1984. *Stories, Scripts, and Scenes: Aspects of Schema Theory.* Hillsdale, N.J.: Erlbaum.

Meyers, M. 1988. "Comments on Literacy." Paper presented at meeting of California Teachers of English. Asilomar Conference Center, Pacific Grove, Calif. March 13.

National Academy of Education. 1985. *Becoming a Nation of Readers.* Washington, D.C.: National Institutes of Education.

O'Connor, F. 1957. *Mystery and Manners.* New York: Farrar, Straus and Giroux.

Petersen, Bruce, ed. 1988. *Convergences: Transactions in Reading and Writing.* Urbana, Ill.: National Council of Teachers of English.

Powell, A., E. Farrar, and D. Cohen. 1985. *The Shopping Mall High School: Winners and Losers in the Educational Marketplace.* Boston: Houghton Mifflin.

Purves, A., ed. 1975. *How Porcupines Make Love: Notes on a Response-centered Curriculum.* Lexington, Mass.: Xerox Publishing.

Ravitch, D., and C. Finn. 1987. *What Do Our 17-year-olds Know?: A Report on the First National Assessment of History and Literature.* New York: Harper and Row.

Resnick, D. P., and L. Resnick. 1977. "The Nature of Literacy: An Historical Explanation." *Harvard Educational Review* 47(3): 370–85.

Resnick, L. 1987. *Education and Learning to Think.* Washington, D.C.: National Academy Press.

Richards, I. A. 1925. *Principles of Literary Criticism.* New York: Harcourt, Brace and World.

Rosenblatt, L. M. 1976. *Literature as Exploration.* New York: Noble and Noble.

——.1978. *The Reader, the Text, the Poem: The Transactional Theory of the Literary Work.* Carbondale: Southern Illinois University Press.

Rumelhart, D. E. 1975. "Notes on a Schema for Stories." In *Representation and Understanding: Studies in Cognitive Science,* ed. D. G. Bobrow and A. Collins. New York: Academic Press.

Scholes, R. 1985. *Textual Power.* New Haven, Conn.: Yale University Press.

Scribner, S., and M. Cole. 1983. *The Psychology of Literacy.* Cambridge, Mass.: Harvard University Press.

Searle, J. 1969. *Speech Acts.* New York: Cambridge University Press.

Slatoff, W. J. 1970. *With Respect to Readers: Dimensions of Literary Response.* Ithaca, N.Y.: Cornell University Press.

Smith, F. 1975. *Understanding Reading.* New York: Holt, Rinehart and Winston.

Squires, James, ed. 1988. *The Dynamics of Language Learning: Research in Reading and English.* Urbana, Ill.: National Council of Teachers of English.

Sternberg, R. J. 1987. "Questioning and Intelligence." *Questioning Exchange* 1(1): 11–14.

Weir, R. 1962. *Language in the Crib.* The Hague: Mouton.

Winner, E. 1982. *Invented Worlds: The Psychology of the Arts.* Cambridge, Mass.: Harvard University Press.

——.1988. *The Point of Words.* Cambridge, Mass.: Harvard University Press.

Wolf, D. 1987. "The Art of Questioning." *Academic Connections.* Winter. New York: College Entrance Examination Board.